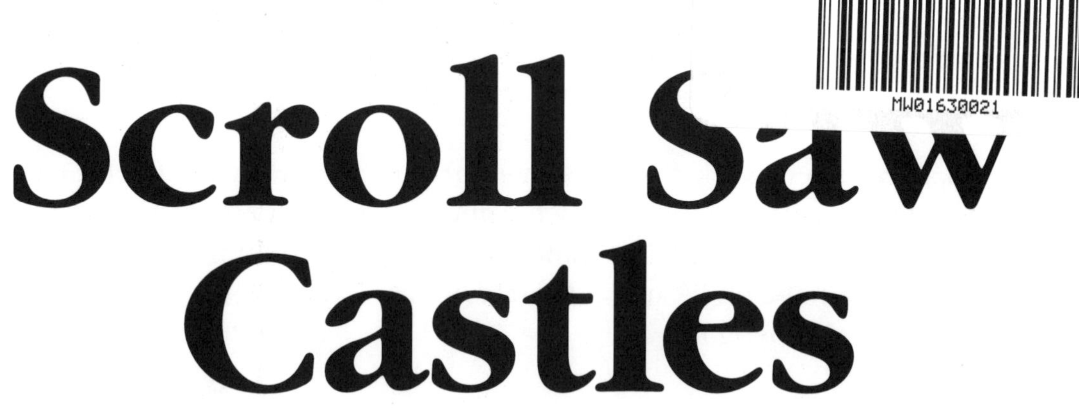

Scroll Saw Castles

How to Make Collapsible Castles on Your Scroll Saw

by Jim Stirling

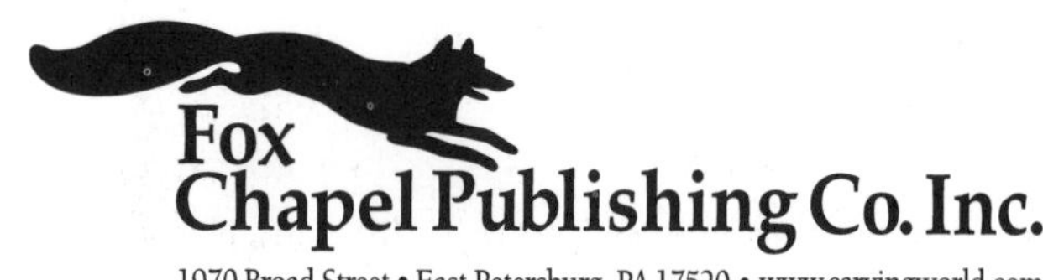

Fox Chapel Publishing Co. Inc.

1970 Broad Street • East Petersburg, PA 17520 • www.carvingworld.com

Copyright ©2001, Fox Chapel Publishing Company, Inc.

Scroll Saw Castles is a brand new work, first published in 2001 by Fox Chapel Publishing Company, Inc. The patterns contained herein are copyrighted by the author. Artists may make three copies of these patterns for personal use and may make any number of projects based on these patterns. The patterns themselves, however, are not to be duplicated for resale or distribution under any circumstances. Any such copying is a violation of copyright laws.

Publisher: Alan Giagnocavo
Project Editor: Ayleen Stellhorn
Desktop Specialist: Linda L. Eberly, Eberly Designs Inc.

ISBN 1-56523-135-X
Library of Congress Card Number 00-110649

To order your copy of this book,
please send check or money order
for the cover price plus $3.00 shipping to:
Fox Books
1970 Broad Street
East Petersburg, PA 17520

Or visit us on the web at
www.foxchapelpublishing.com

Manufactured in the USA

Because the operation of woodworking equipment inherently includes the risk of injury and damage, this book cannot guarantee that creating the projects in this book is safe for everyone. For this reason, this book is sold without warranties or guarantees of any kind, express or implied, and the Publisher and Authors disclaim any liability for any injuries, losses or damages caused in any way by the content of this book or the reader's operation of woodworking equipment. The publisher and the author urge all woodworkers to thoroughly review each project and to understand the operation of any woodworking equipment involved before beginning any project presented here.

TABLE OF CONTENTS

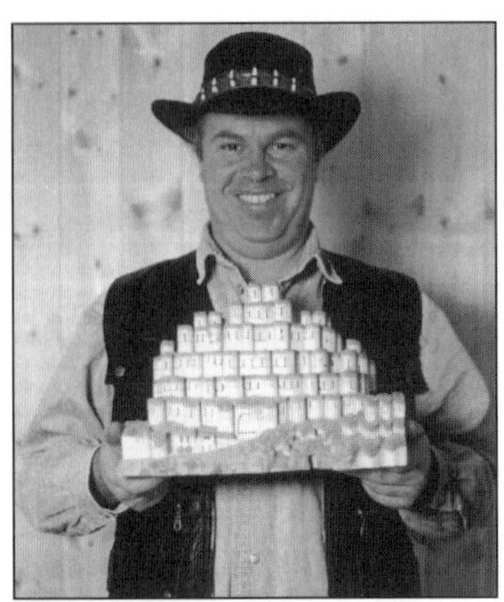

Author Jim Stirling and one example of his scroll-sawed castles.

This book started, perhaps, when I was thirteen years old in North Queensland, Australia. I saw a film in which Kirk Douglas was a Viking out to conquer England. The film was full of beautiful blondes. These Nordic ladies made a very strong impression on this pubescent teenager, and I decided then and there that one day I would travel to Norway.

So when I was about 25, I left Australia's shores on a hiking world trip. Wherever I visited, I went to church. Not that I could understand much of the languages, but I had the sincere hope of being invited home for lunch after the services. I would stand there with the pastor, looking like an endangered species, and greet all, especially those who looked like they could cook. Well, up in Narvik, Norway, a lady felt sorry for me. She had a daughter. We became pen pals.

Part of my trip took me to Scotland. While there, I picked up a basic model of a wooden castle that had been made in Switzerland. I became inspired by this technique of making conical towers to form a castle and began to make my own castles. The first one I made, I sent to my Norwegian pen pal with a note that said, "Princess Edel, you've got the castle. All you need now is Prince Charming!" The castle did the trick. She came down to Australia for a visit.

I was, by now, making castles and selling them at the Kuranda markets of North Queensland, Australia. Busy making a castle on the scroll saw with my admirer beside me, I made the suggestion to Edel, without looking up, "Edel, how about we get married?" She took a long while to reply, but by the time I finished the castle she said that it sounded like a pretty good idea. I burned a message on the bottom of the castle: "To my princess on our engagement day."

She returned home and I worked flat-out on the scroll saw to earn money for my passage to Norway. In Australia, the scroll saw is called a fret saw, and a local newspaper wrote an article about me and my work during that time entitled "Fretting for his Fiancee!" Months later, Edel and I were married in the middle of Oslo fjord on board the *Anne Rogde,* oldest schooner in the world.

Now that I think about it, this book may have started even further back when I was a toddler. I grew up in the middle of a rainforest in North Queensland, Australia. My Dad was a National Parks ranger. Mum was an artist. Right from the start, they encouraged me to make things with my hands. I developed my creativity along with my knowledge and love of the jungle. I give them much of the honor for my abilities with wood, and for my rich fantasy.

My name is Stirling, so I make "Stirling Castles," though there is an age-old castle by this name in a town in Scotland. My plan for this book is to describe, in detail, the process I use to make my castles and other models. Who knows, it might be the beginning of a fairy tale for you as well!

GALLERY

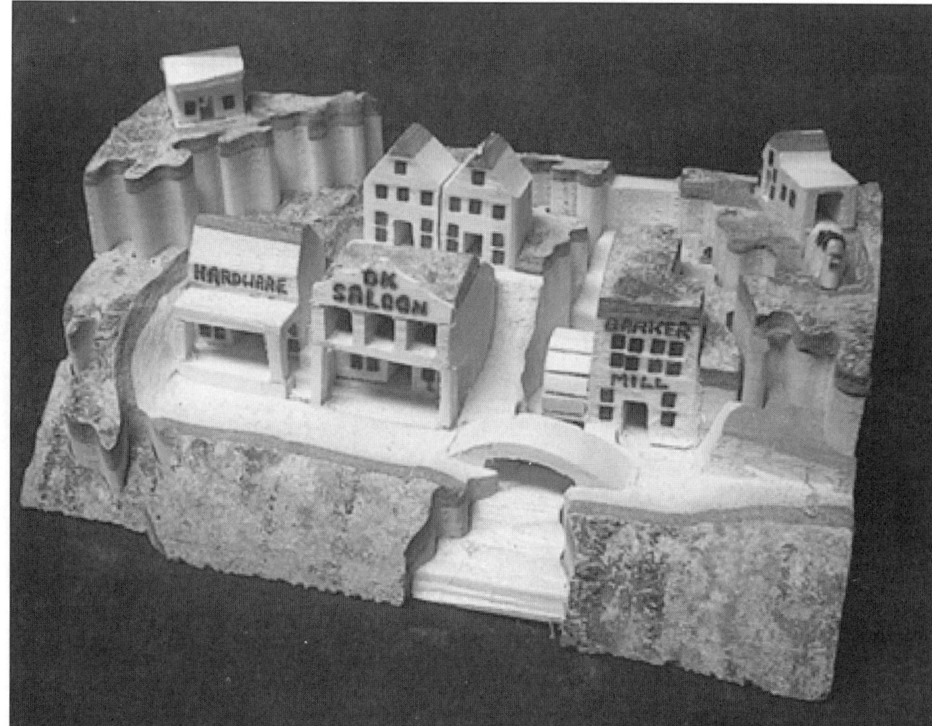

Bodie,
page 52

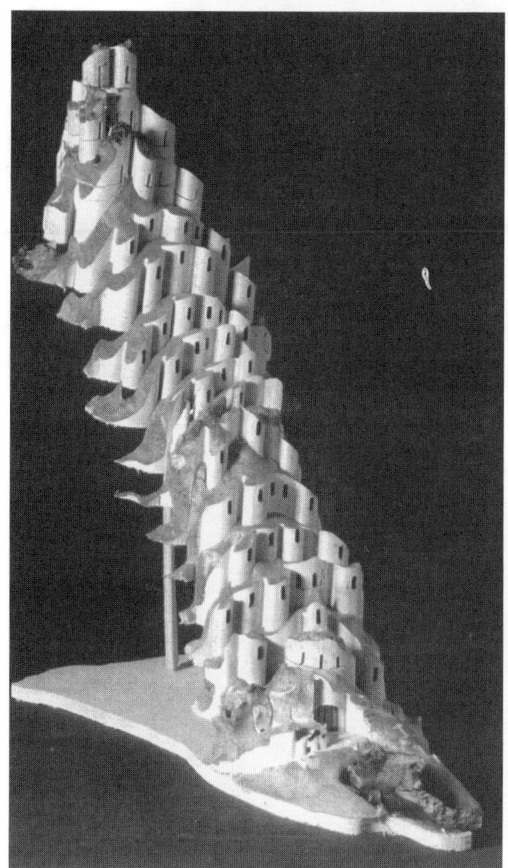

Castle Rock

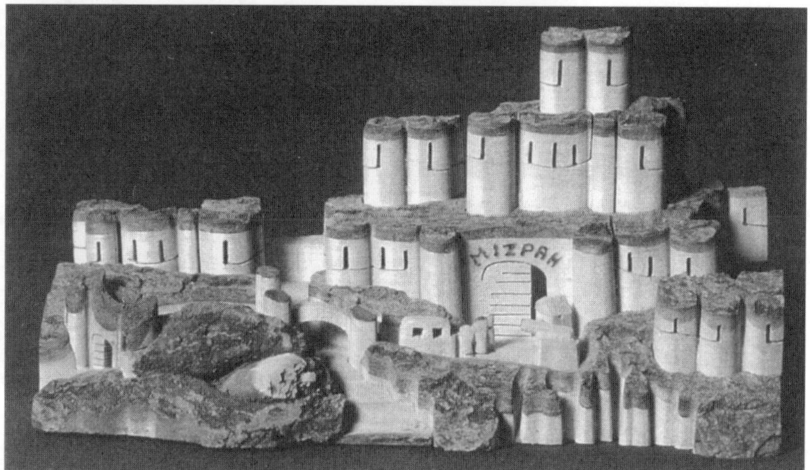

Mother-in-Law's
Castle, page 19

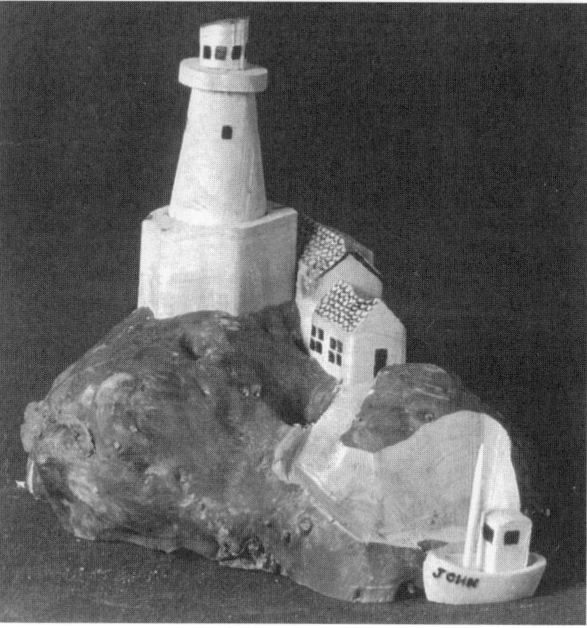

Lighthouse

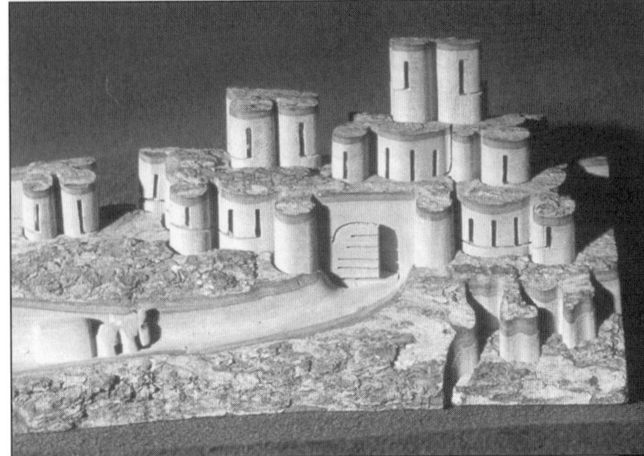

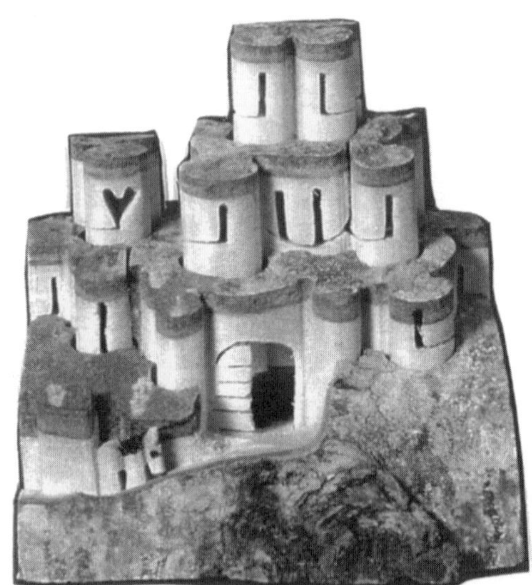

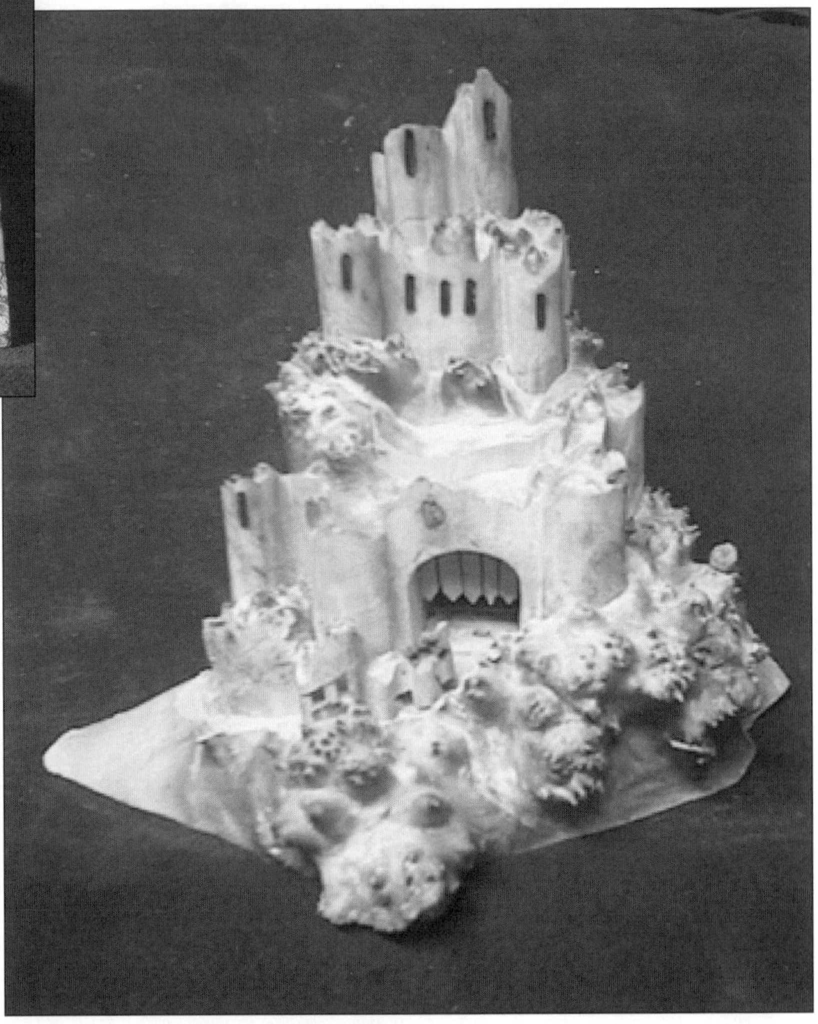

Burl Castle, page 23

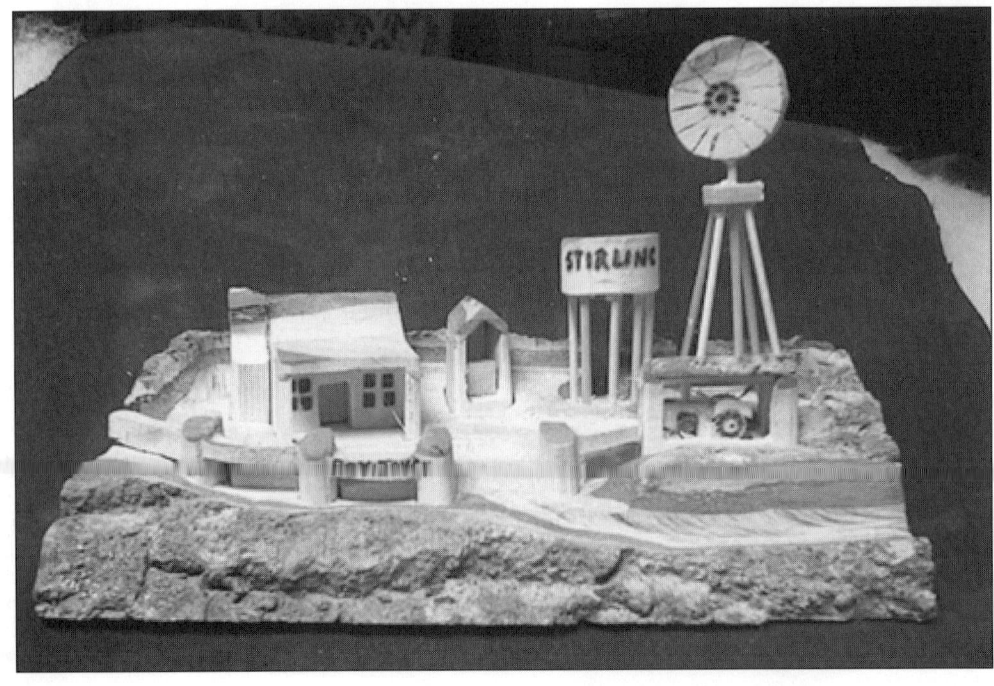

Aussy Farm, page 33

SCROLL SAW CASTLES

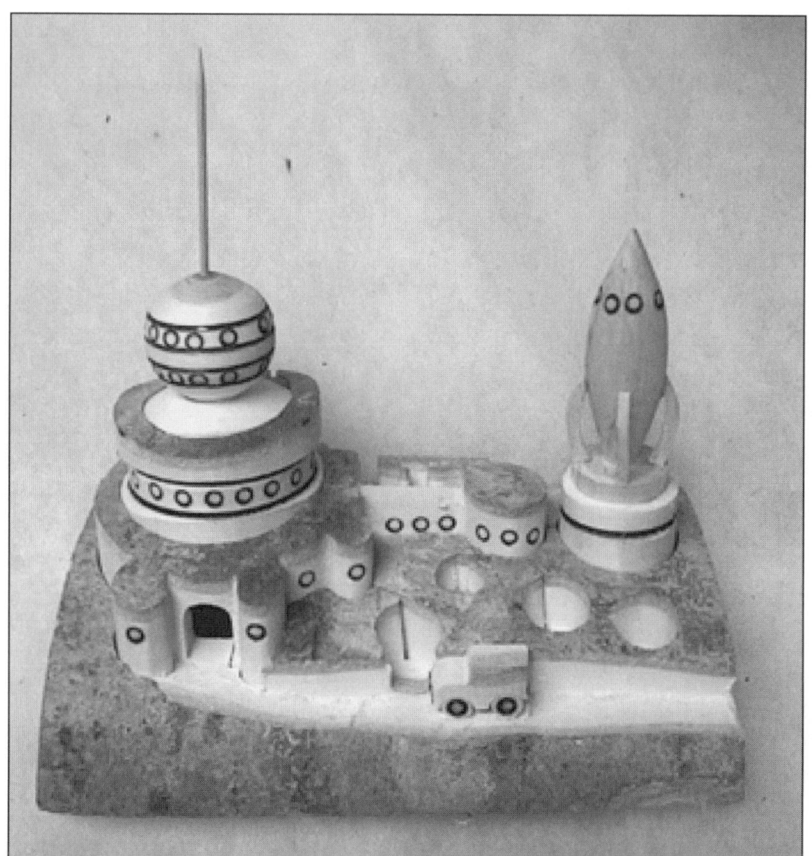

Moon Colony, page 57

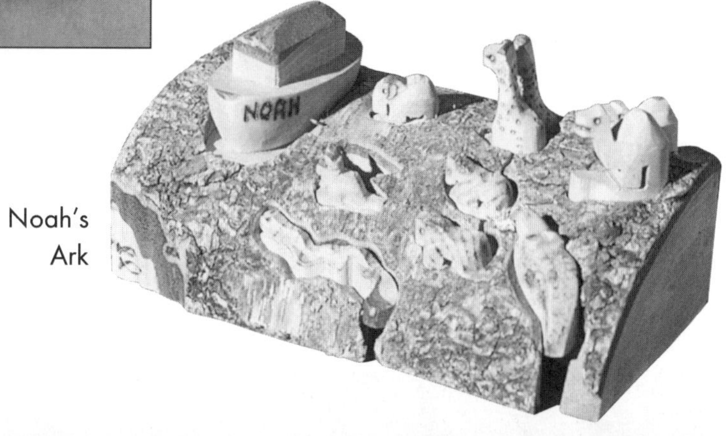

Norway Church, page 54

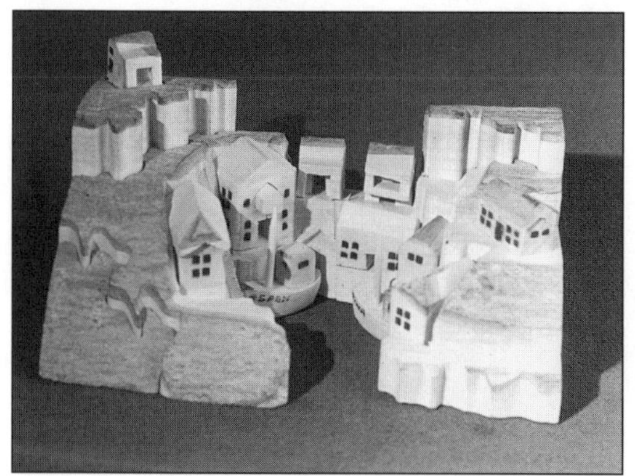

Norwegian Fishing Village, page 39

Noah's Ark

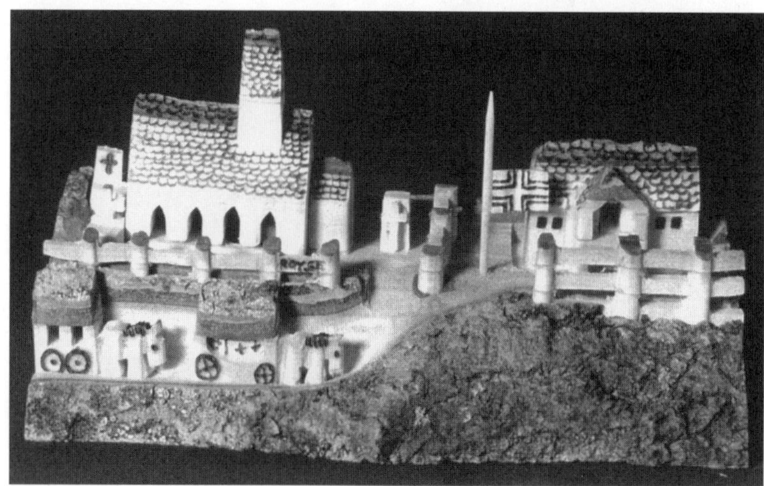

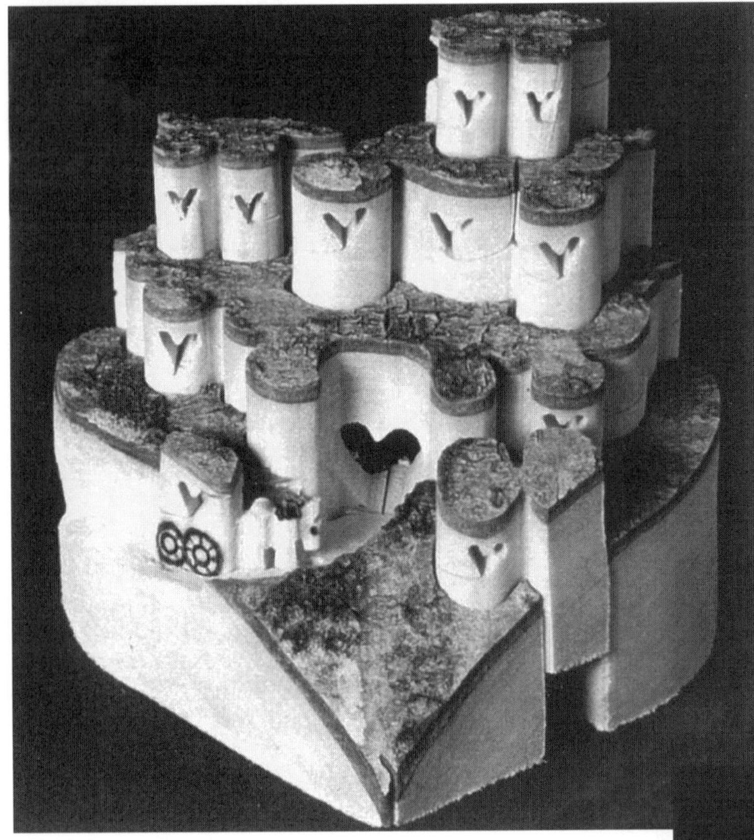

Heart Castle, page 44

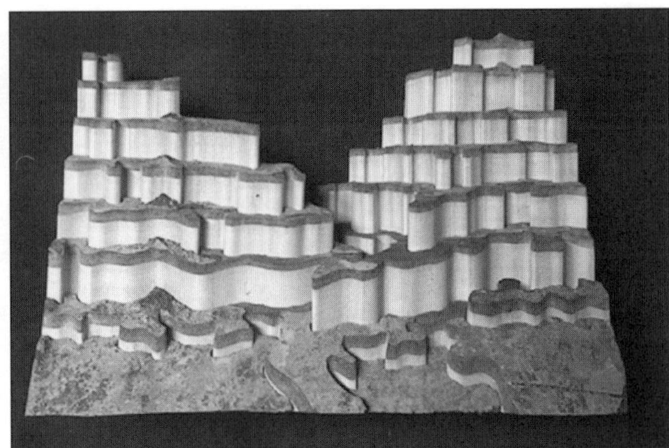

Grand Canyon

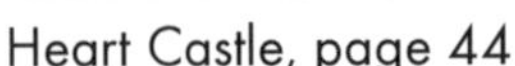

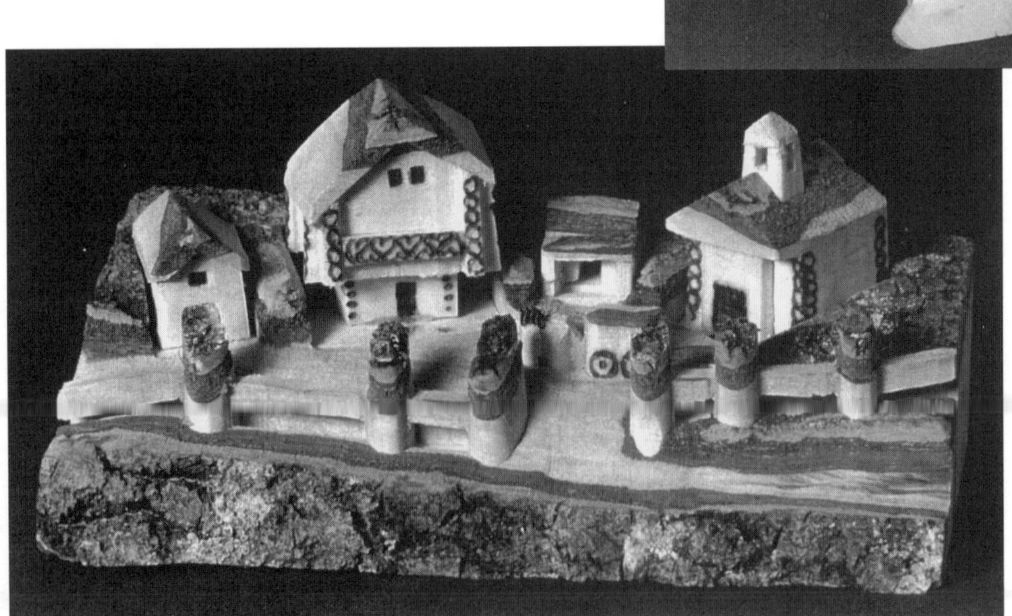

Norway Farm House
(variation), page 30

TIPS & TECHNIQUES

CHOOSING AND CUTTING WOOD

Because I use wood that is as thick as a scroll saw can handle, it is important that I use a fairly soft wood. My wood of choice is aspen wood. It is white and soft. The bark tends to stick to the wood, and where I live in Norway, it is readily available. When I am in Australia, I use camphor laurel. Many of the soft woods that you regularly use in America on the scroll saw will work well. I have limited experience cutting American woods, but ash seems to cut fine, as does poplar. Birch is a good choice, but a bit on the hard side.

I usually fell a tree and cut it into chest-high pieces. I cut off the small limbs a couple of inches from the trunk. These can be used for interesting highlights to the castles.

When I get home, I cut the wood lengthwise

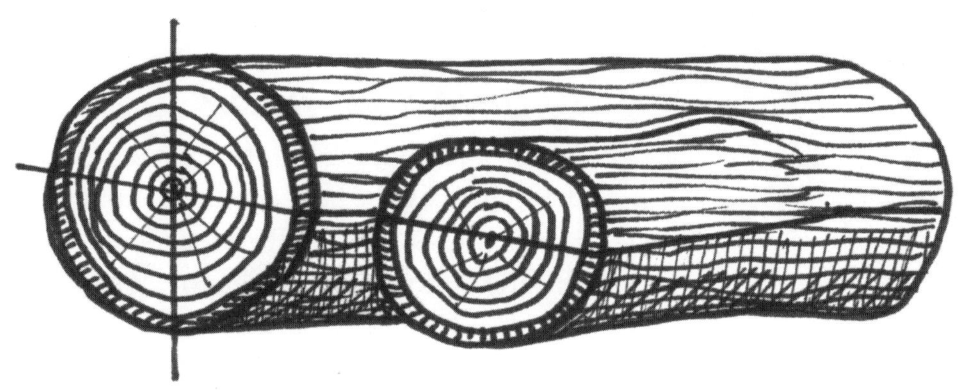

Larger logs should be cut into quarters to dry. Smaller logs and branches should be cut in half.

through the middle and then on the quarter. I stand these pieces in a warm place to dry.

When dry, I use a bandsaw to cut the pieces to a smaller size. The cutting height of most scroll saws is about two inches. I cut the pieces about two inches high, two-and-a-half to six inches wide, and four inches to 12 inches long (5 cm by 6 to 15 cm by 10 to 30 cm). I then sand these pieces on a belt sander, so the back of the wood is perpendicular to the base.

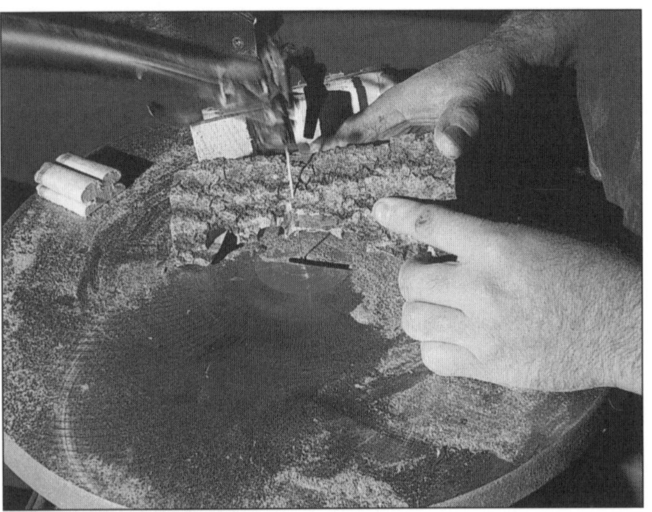

Scroll saws are limited in the height of wood that they can cut. I cut logs down on a bandsaw so they are small enough to fit under the blade of my scroll saw.

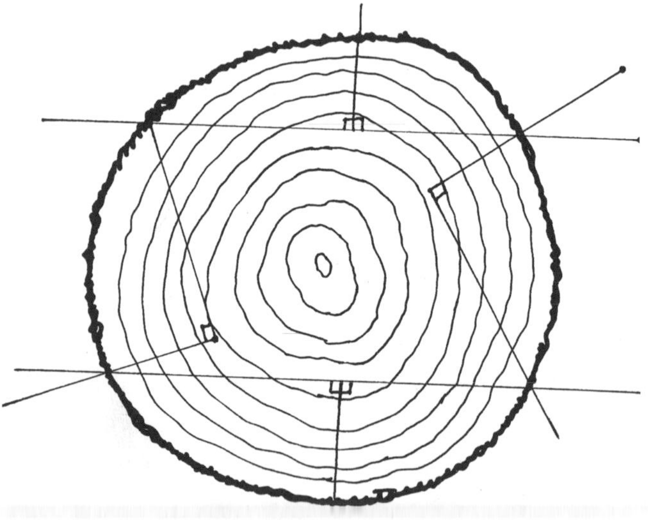

This diagram shows one way to cut a log into smaller, more manageable pieces for use on the scroll saw. The bark side of the wood becomes the top of the castle, while the cut sides become the bottom and back of the castle.

BURLS

Many trees have small burls on them, which make very interesting castles. It is good to collect burls in the springtime when the bark is easier to remove. Take a backpack, two axes and a bow saw on a trip into the forest. Be sure you have the landowner's permission to collect burls and never take burls from state or national forests.

To remove a burl, make a cut horizontally on the trunk, a few inches above the burl. Make another cut a few inches below the burl. Place one axe vertically on the trunk, just behind the burl. Hit the back of the axe blade with the back of the other axe. The burl should break straight off. This creates little disturbance to the tree—and to anyone who might own it.

Burls often look best with the bark removed. The burl can be boiled in water, which makes the bark easier to loosen. The best method is to use a high pressure water cleaner. I use a turbo tip on the cleaner, which ejects the water in a spiralling pattern. Just put on a pair of gumboots and stand on the burl. Hold the nozzle of the sprayer so that it is almost touching the wood. The bark just can't resist the pressure and will come right off. Let the burls dry slowly in a warm place before you cut them on the scroll saw.

GLUING THE BARK

With camphor laurel in Australia, I have found that removing the bark and then gluing it back on is best. I use a fairly dull kitchen knife and slide it in between the bark and the wood on one edge of the block. I work the knife lengthwise around the block. Often the whole piece of bark will just pop off. I then spread a standard white wood glue on the wood and inside the bark. I bind the bark back on with elastic bands and let the glue dry completely. Give the block a final sanding to remove any excess glue.

CHOOSING A SCROLL SAW

I am currently negotiating with my New Zealand inventor/engineer mate Harry to make a "Super scroll saw." Features will include a strong motor, robust construction, ability to cut at least six inches of wood, a variable orbit and a user-friendly attitude. If you would like to know more about my "super scroll saw," contact me and I will send you some information when it is ready.

I have tested saws produced by RBIndustries and DeWalt with good results, and currently use a Delta saw and a Hegner saw in my shop in Norway. Each has its advantages and disadvantages.

Delta: The C-arm gives the saw an aggressive orbital action. The addition of a strong electronic motor makes it a very fast saw. It is suitable for the initial tower-making part of building scroll saw castles.

To obtain the high degree of tension on the blade that I need, I have to push down on the carbon arm. This compromises the height of the piece that I can pass over the blade. The attachment system is rather complicated. Because there is so much space between the oscillating arm and the blade attachment, the sideways travel of the blade is fairly great.

Hegner: The parallel oscillating arms make this saw very accurate. The less aggressive orbit makes the saw excellent for cutting the finer work on the castles, like the doors, windows, horses and carriages. A screw at the back tightens the arms allowing the full length of the blade to be used. and thicker pieces to be cut. The attachment system is simple and reliable, and there is very little sideways movement of the blade.

The best advice on choosing a scroll saw is to talk to other scroll saw users that you know. They will be more than happy to tell you about their experiences with other makes and models. Be sure to "test drive" scroll saws at the store or at a show before you purchase one for use at home.

CHOICE OF BLADES

I use Pebeco no. 12 blades, available from Hegner distributors. This blade gives a fine cut, and the thicker blade allows for the high degree of tension needed to produce the straight cuts in the swings of the castle. I have also tried Olsen blades: Universal no. 12 Olsen 439 double tooth blades, Olsen 453 skip tooth blades, and Olsen 4080 hook tooth blades for thick wood. All of these worked very well when I put them to the test of cutting a castle.

Some blades have backward-facing teeth on the bottom end of the blade. These are suitable for jobs where tearing on the underside can be a problem. When working with such thick wood, these reverse teeth make cutting less effective. A final sanding on an eccentric, band or orbital sander is all that is needed to remove the furry edges.

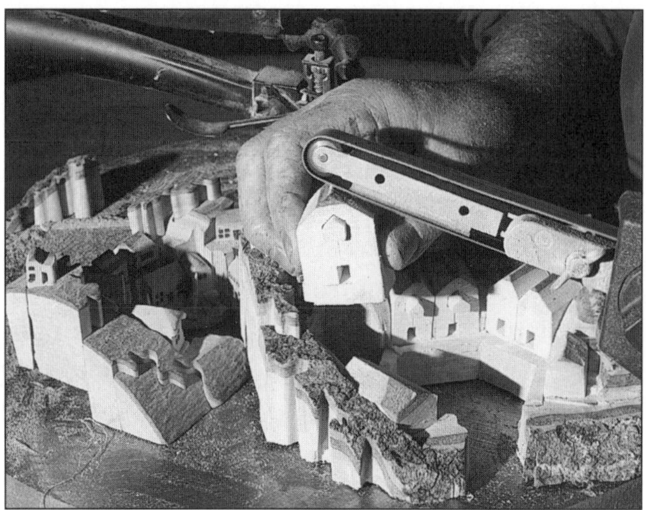

Sanding devices help shape the final pieces. This is one of the shops in the Norwegian fishing village scene.

GENERAL TIPS

Sanding: A belt sander is a good tool for initial block preparation. It can also be used for finishing. In addition, I use an eccentric sander and an orbital sander for finishing.

Repairs: I always have a hot glue gun turned on when I'm working so I can instantly repair bits I've accidentally sawn or broken off. Good old-fashioned white wood glue is effective as well.

Roads: The more complicated castles have a road leading the handsome prince in his carriage up to the gates of his princess' castle. I use a Dremel tool with a high-speed cutter, number 115, to make the road. A sanding drum also is effective.

Shaping: Black and Decker has a "Superfile," which is very useful. It is a sanding machine with a half-inch belt. I use it extensively in road making and shaping the roofs of buildings. It is often easier to get the shape you want, for example on the roof of a building, by using this tool rather than by sawing.

HIGHLIGHTING

Highlighting can be done with a woodburning pen. There are soldering iron types called pyrography pens. These are often supplied with differently shaped tips. One such tip burns a round ring, which is good for making wheels on vehicles and windows on moon homes. In some castles, I use an elongated window-shaped tool that I have ground to shape. For house and building windows, I use a square-tipped iron.

Other systems have a solid state power supply with variable heat control. Razortip, a woodburning system produced in Canada, is one such unit. It has several exchangeable tips. I find the writing tip for signing and shading to be the most useful.

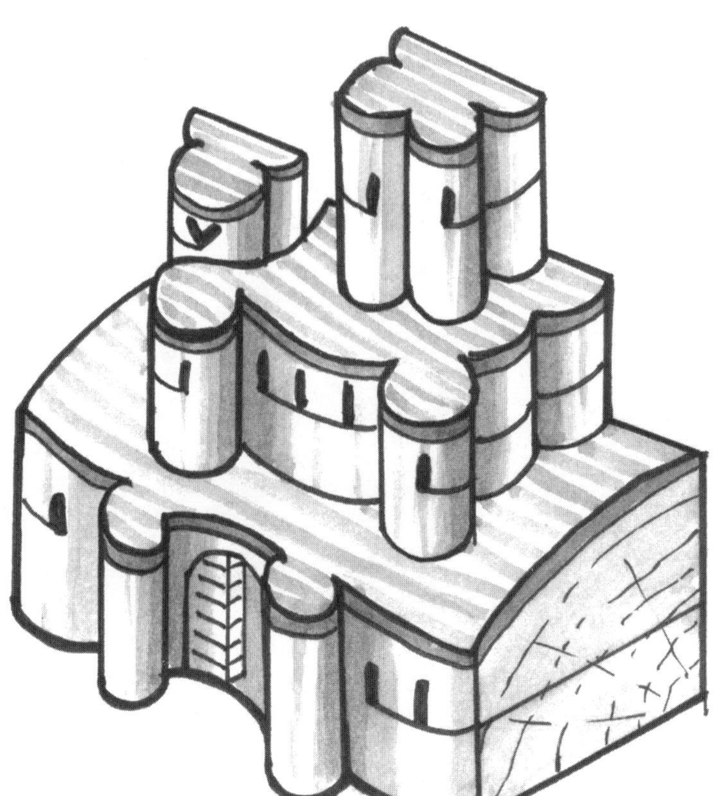

This simple castle has only a few cuts. It is designed to help you get a good start on castle-making.

CUTTING A SIMPLE CASTLE

1. Cut the front of the castle. Make this cut with the saw set at 0 degrees. Strive to make nice, bowed cuts. The walls to the sides of the gates are bowed outward. The gate itself is bowed inward. This will look natural when cutting the gate later. The fronts of the turrets beside the gates come out almost to the front of the wood.

2. Cut the first tower. Set the table at about 1 to 2 degrees (the right-hand side of the table is pushed down). Always start on the right and swing the wood counter-clockwise so the saw cuts clockwise. Start a small cut a little to the right of the center of the wood. Back out and turn the piece around. Test the angle of the cut against the back of the blade. (This is a good way to test if your table is level as well.) Line the right-hand side of the blade up with the left-hand side of the cut at the top of the wood. Look at the bottom of the cut. The left-hand side of the blade should line up with right-hand side of the cut. If this has confused you, just start and make a cut. It's only a bit of wood anyway!

Cut into the wood, swinging in a nice counter-clockwise arc, about 90 degrees, until the wood is length-wise with the saw. Make a place to turn the blade by first stopping the forward cutting pressure, then jiggling the wood first clockwise, then counter-clockwise. Turn the piece clockwise around the blade about 180 degrees. Now you are cutting out in the direction that you cut in.

Cut counter-clockwise, about 270 degrees, in a nice arc until the front of the piece is facing away from you. Jiggle the wood again, then turn the wood, 180 degrees clockwise. Make another arc, similar to the first 270 degrees. The wood is now lengthwise to the blade and the cut looks like a clover leaf. Swing clockwise another 180 degrees and cut an arc out to the back of the wood.

Test how high the tower slides up. If it doesn't slide up enough, repeat the cut. Pull up on the tower as you are cutting. This will narrow the space between the two pieces. You will feel the tower ris-

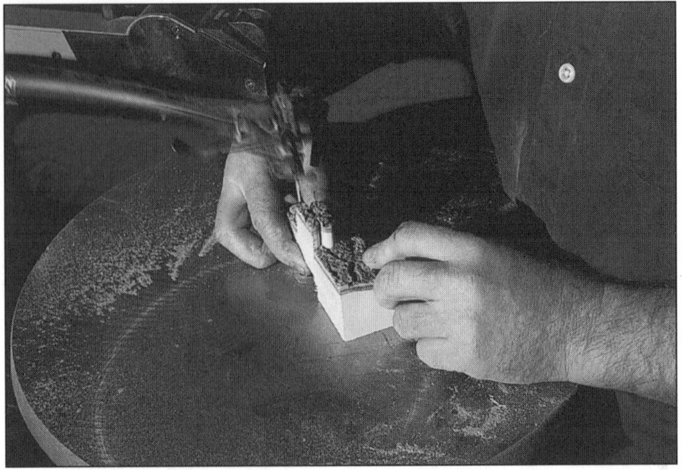

Recutting the first tower to bring it up to proper height. Note my index finger is pushing the piece up to make a tighter line for the saw blade to follow. Be careful not to cut your fingers!

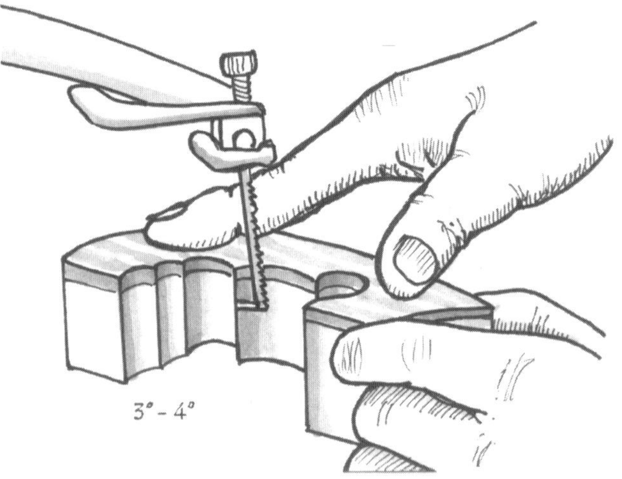

3° - 4°

If a piece slips right through, set the saw table at about four degrees and cut a sliver off the next piece. Glue this to the front bottom part of the tower.

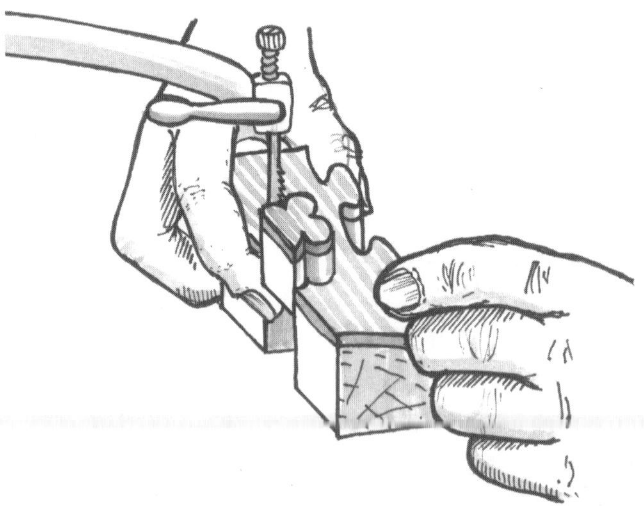

If after cutting the first tower it doesn't come up far enough, you can widen the cut by going through the cut again while pushing the piece up as shown.

ing as you follow the first cut. When you feel the tower has been raised enough, push it down again and cut your way out carefully without cutting too much more off the sides. If you want to raise the tower still more, repeat this process again. A word of warning. Do not widen the cut too much. Remember, the blade itself will stop the tower rising as far as it will when you are finished the cut.

If the tower pushes up and right through the wood, you didn't have enough angle on your table. This can be repaired in several ways. Remove the offending tower, the set the table at about 4 degrees. Take the piece of wood from which the tower was removed and cut an arc around the bottom of the area without cutting the top of wood. You will be left with a small half-moon-shaped wedge. Glue this wedge to the bottom of the removed turret with your glue gun.

You can change the height by adjusting how far this wedge extends up from the bottom of the turret. Push the tower up to a suitable height, then insert the wedge from underneath. Push the wedge in until it is tight. Make a pencil mark where the inside of the wedge meets the tower. Remove the tower and glue the wedge into position. Cut any excess of the wedge so it is flush with the bottom of the castle.

Alternately, you can put glue on the inside of the

wedge, then push both the tower and the wedge into place and let them dry. When the glue is dry, remove the tower and cut off any excess. Another way is to glue the wedge in place and sand it until it fits correctly.

3. Cut the second terrace. Tilt the table a little more than the one to two degrees at which it is currently set. (This piece will extend into the thinner wood at the front of the block, so you need a little more angle to stop the cut piece from extending too far up.) Start the cut to the right side of the first tower. Follow the line shown in the drawing.

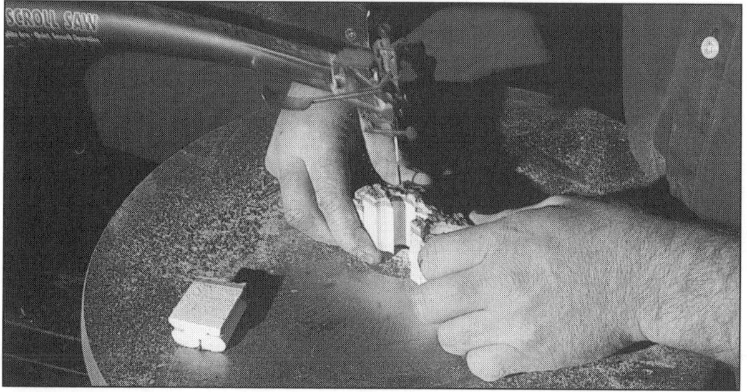

Recutting the second terrace to bring it up to the right height.

4. Cut the princess' tower. Start the cut to the left of the exit of the second terrace cut. Make just one turret. Finish the cut by exiting out the side of the piece.

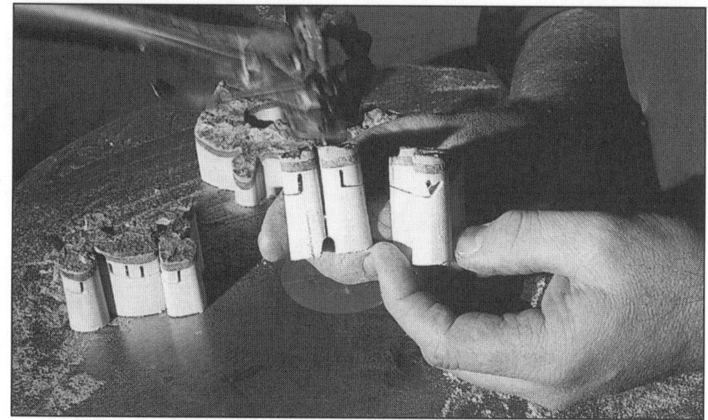

Completed towers of the Simple Castle.

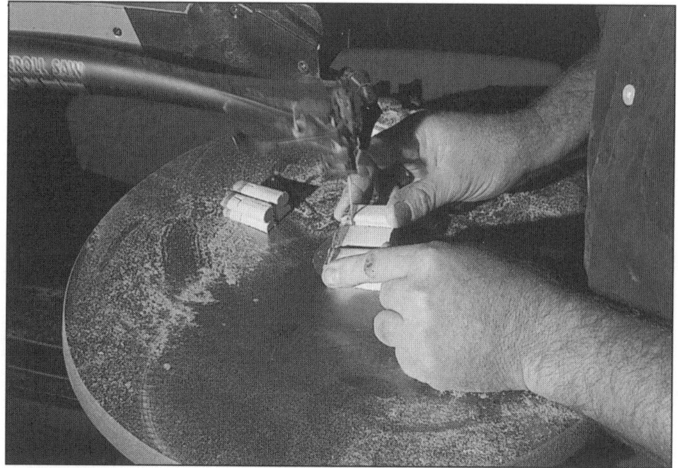

Cutting the windows in the second terrace. In an attempt to make the cut as inconspicuous as possible, the saw is introduced in the crevice between the towers.

5. Cut the windows. Take the first tower and lay it down on its back. Cut a slightly bowed cut in from one side. Extend the cut to slightly farther than the center of the turret. Back up a little and swing the tower sharply 90 degrees, so you are cutting toward the top of the piece. Try to cut parallel to the walls of the turret. Reverse back down to the insertion cut, then swing back 90 degrees. Move forward into the extended cut and swing sharply, 90 degrees back again. Cut beside the first cut to form an elongated bow-shooters window. Round the top of the cut in a nice arch. Back out along the entrance cut. To make windows in the other turret, start in from the other side of the piece.

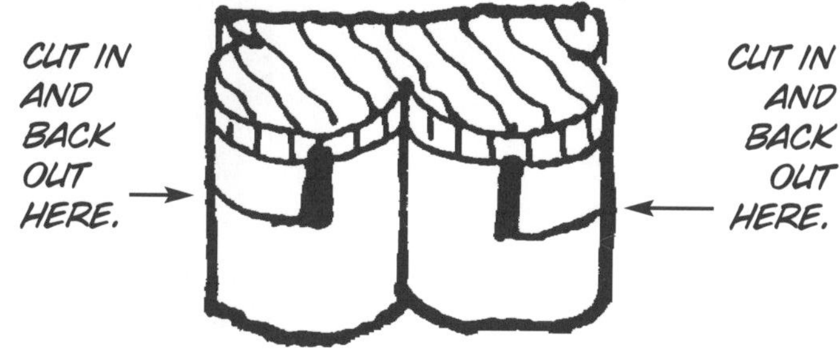

6. Cut windows in the second turret. Lay the piece on its back and cut windows in from each side.

The windows in the middle section are made by sawing down from the top of the terrace, along where you have cut sharply out of a tower. (See the illustration on page 13.) This helps to make the cut a little more inconspicuous. Bow the horizontal cut downward to match the swing formed where the bark meets the wood. Cut three windows in this middle section.

7. Cut the heart window. The princess' tower is decorated with a heart-shaped window. Two windows placed at right angles to each other create the heart.

8. Cut the windows and gate at the front. Cut in from each side and make two or three windows on both sides of the building next to the gate. I don't usually cut windows in the turrets right beside the gate. To cut the gate, cut up from the bottom and bow the cut over at the top. The bow should match the bow between the bark and the wood. I usually make a gate that appears to be slid half-way shut. (See the illustration on page 13.)

9. Put the castle together. Sand the bottom and back with the towers down. Sign your name on the bottom.

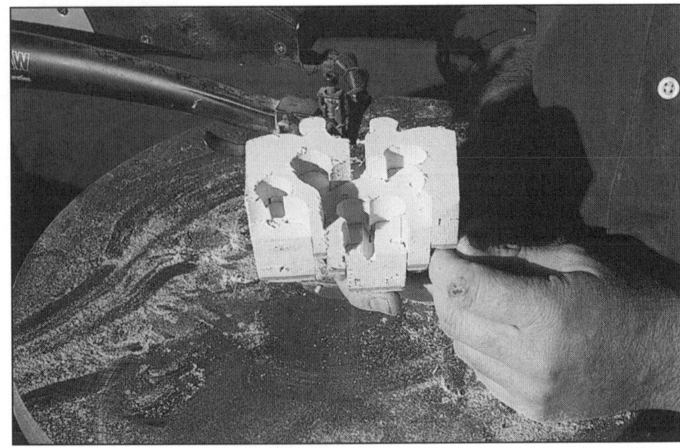

A photo of the completed castle, turned upside down with all the pieces in the raised position.

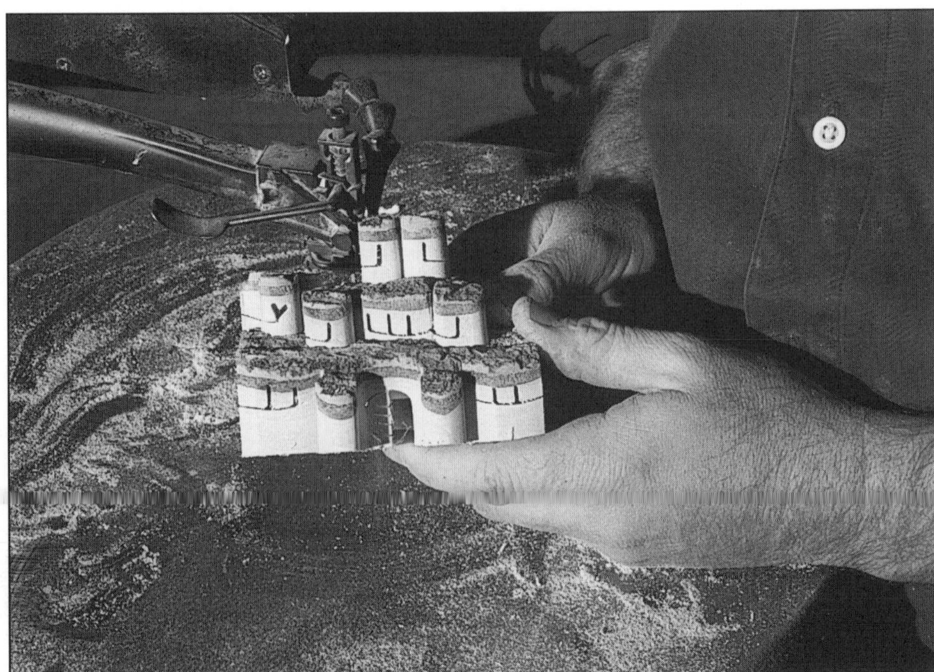

The completed castle, still warm from cutting. The saw cuts so cleanly that sanding is necessary only on the underside of the pieces.

SIMPLE CASTLE

PLAN ELEVATION

PIECES EXTENDING
INTO THINNER
WOOD NEED
MORE ANGLE
THAN PIECES IN
THICKER WOOD.

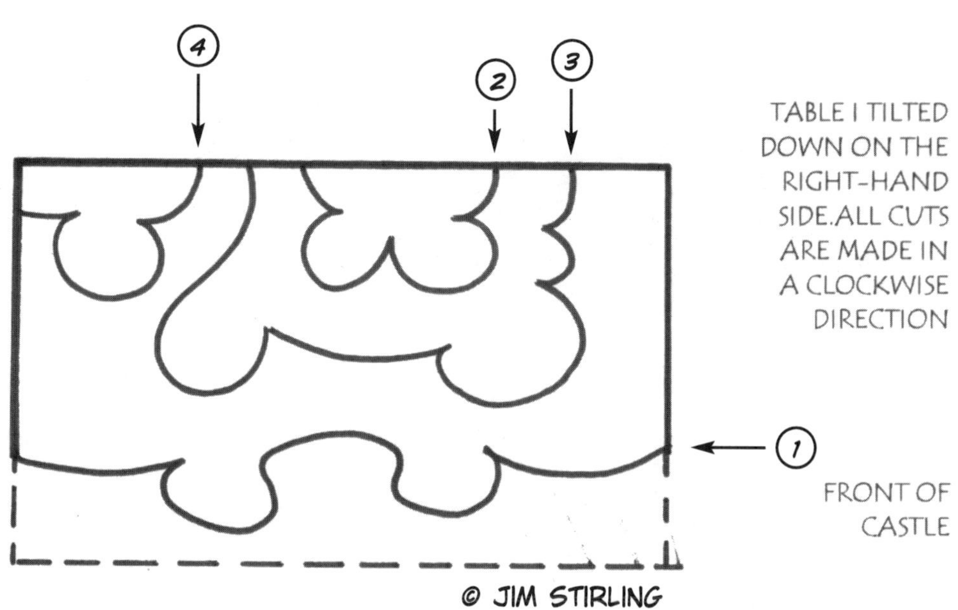

TABLE I TILTED
DOWN ON THE
RIGHT-HAND
SIDE. ALL CUTS
ARE MADE IN
A CLOCKWISE
DIRECTION

FRONT OF
CASTLE

© JIM STIRLING

HEART SHAPE
IS TWO WINDOWS
AT RIGHT ANGLES.

FRONT ELEVATION

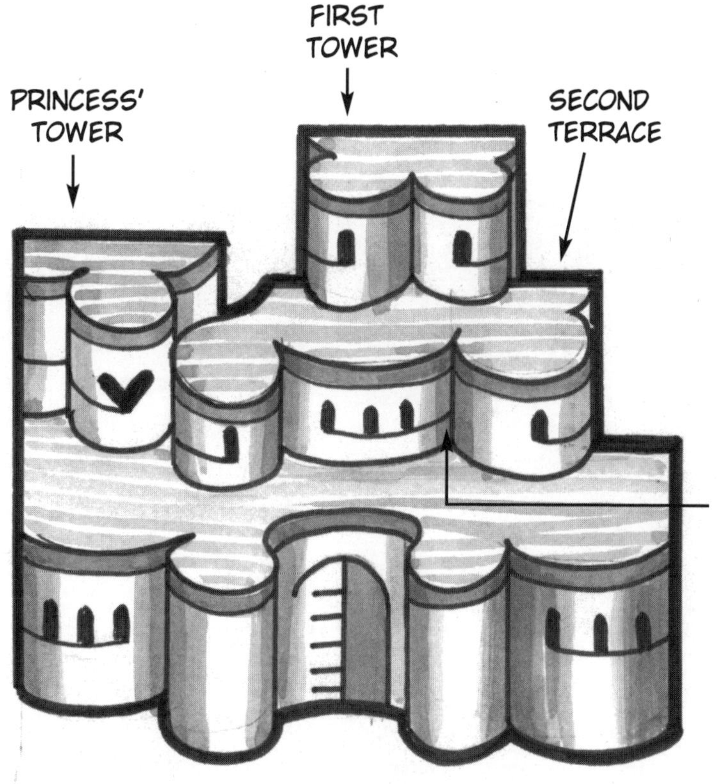

TO CUT WINDOWS
IN THE MIDDLE
SECTION, SAW IN
ALONG JOINT
IN TURRETS.

Note: The entrance
cut to the central
window in the second
terrace can be made
less conspicuous by
sawing down the
crevice between the
towers.

Cuts into windows
follow concave or
convex lines of the
bark above.

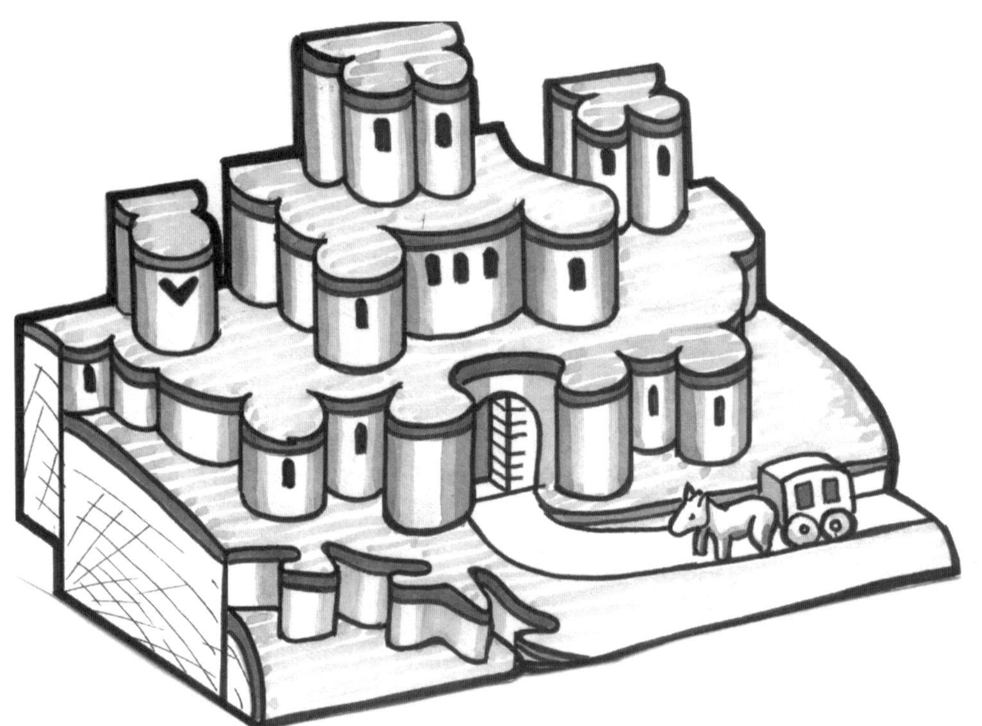

Make a princess castle complete with a handsome prince. A dashing white steed is bringing the prince's coach up the mountain road to propose!

PRINCESS CASTLE

This project is suited to a larger piece of wood. The diagrams that follow need to be enlarged to represent actual size. When completed, the castle measures seven inches long, three-and-a-half inches wide and two inches tall (18cm by 9cm by 5 cm).

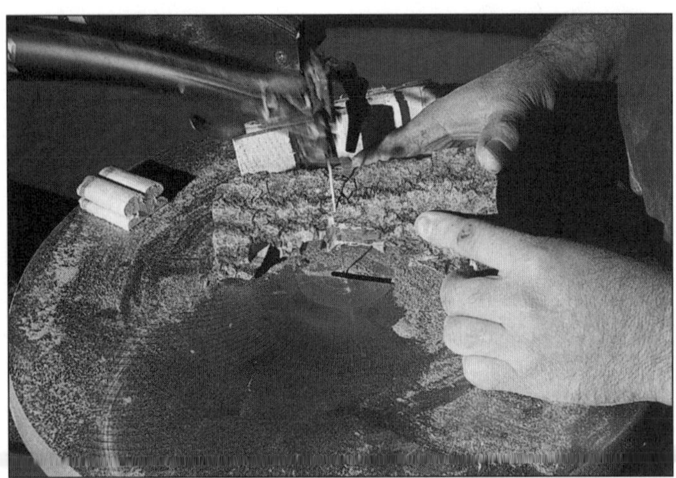

To form the entrance to the castle gate, place the piece on its back and cut out a trough shape piece. The piece may be too high o cut with the saw. The trough must then be routed or sanded out.

Set the saw at about 1 degree. Start by making the towers at the back of the castle. Then move on to the second terrace, increasing the tilt of the table a little more.

Third terrace: The third terrace forms the front of the castle. Cut in from the side of the piece. This cut must be started or finished not more than 3/8 in. (1cm) from the back of the wood, otherwise the whole castle will topple over backwards when completed.

Gate: When the third terrace is cut and rises up to the required height, remove the pieces. Take the front piece of wood—the land in front of the castle—and cut a threshold to the gate. Place the piece on its back and cut out a trough-shaped piece. The bottom

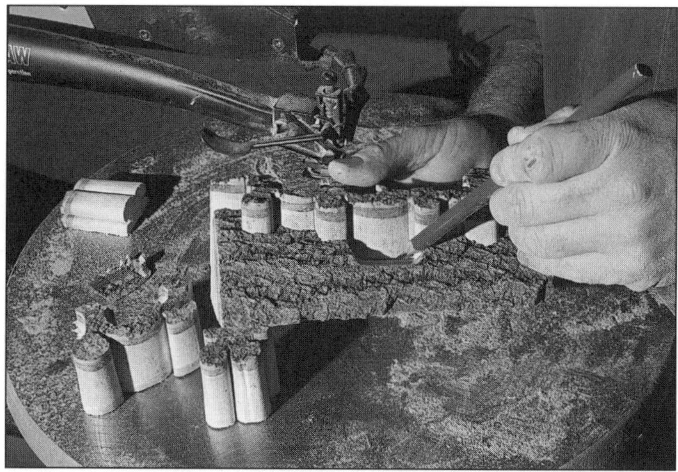

Push the third terrace up into place in the front piece of the castle. Make a pencil mark along the trough shaped cut you made. This marks the bottom of the gate. Remove the third terrace and cut out the gate.

of this piece runs parallel to the base of the wood. Leave about 3/4 in. to 1 1/4 in. (2 to 3 cm) of wood. Set the third terrace back and move it up until it stops. Make a pencil mark along where the threshold meets the gate. Draw a suitable gate. Remove the terrace and cut out the gate, starting in from the bottom. Cut along the line you have drawn to mark the bottom of the gate.

Horse and carriage: The horse and carriage is made in the thinner wood at the front of the castle.

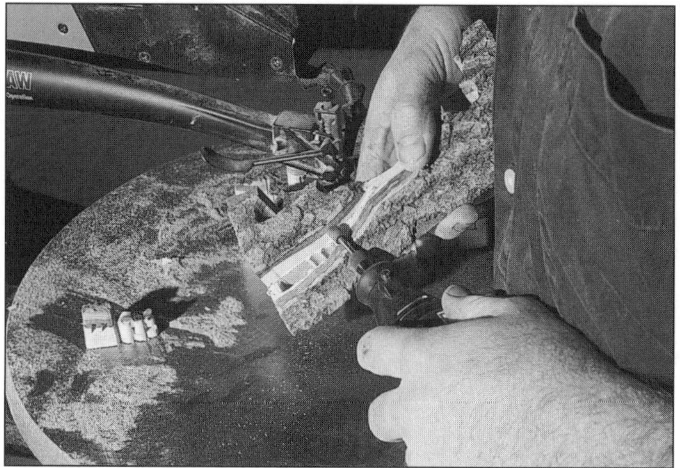

Make the horse and carriage first, then shape the road with a sanding drum, router or chisel. By trial and error, keep cutting the road down until, when inserting the horse, the road passes just under the horse's feet.

It is best to do this cut before making the road. Set the table at about 4 degrees and follow the pattern shown on page 15. It is a rather intricate shape that takes a bit of practice. If you want a horse with its head up, then make the head and neck section longer when cutting the bird's eye profile. Take the piece out. Slow the saw down to make the details in the horizontal dimension. Begin the cut under the horse's feet.

Road: Now make the road. I use Dremel tool with high-speed cutter number 115. A sanding drum will work well also. Keep on cutting the road away until it goes just under the level of the horse's feet when he is inserted.

Cliff: A cliff face can be made opposite the horse to bring interest to the front of the piece. Again, set the table at 4 degrees, right-hand side of the table down. If you are making a cliff on the right-hand side of the castle, you must start the cut in from the side of the wood and exit on the left-hand side of the wood. This assures that the cliff tightens as it moves down, not up. Make the cut as meandering as possi-

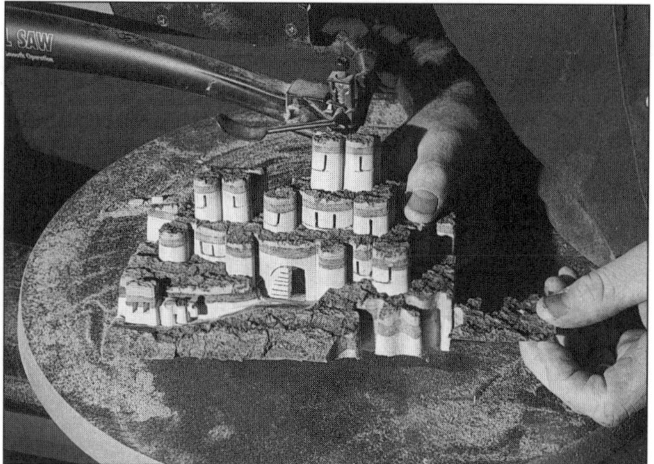

Make a cliff at the front of the castle. Put the table on about four degrees, and starting in from the right hand side of the castle, make a tortuous cut down to the front of the piece. The piece will slide down. Make a pencil mark on the excess. If you are making a cliff face on the left side of the castle, you will need to start the cut at the front of the castle and proceed to the left hand side of the piece.

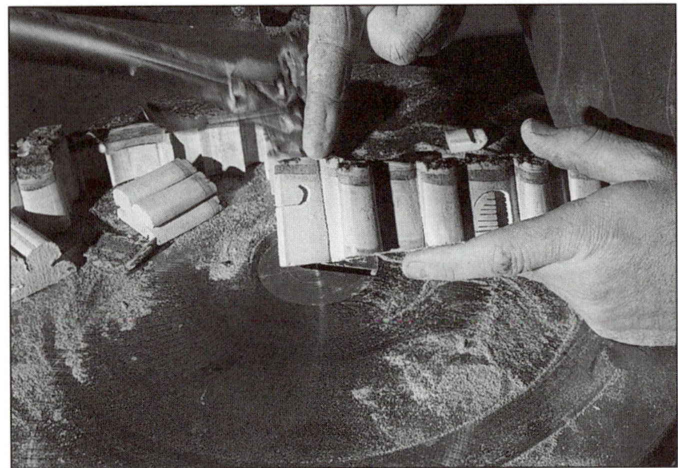

Windows can give a hint as to the function of the room behind them. This window indicates a very important, though lesser throne room in every castle.

pencil. Remove the cliff piece, lay it on its back and cut off the excess that was protruding down below the base. The base of the piece will be parallel to the blade when placed on the right-hand side of the blade. So as to cut the excess away at the proper angle, always have the base of the cliff on the left-hand side as you cut.

The length of the piece will determine the number of towers you can make along the back of the castle. The width of the piece determines how many terraces the piece will have. If the width of the front terrace is too wide however, it will be too high when placed on its back to cut out the windows. This can be corrected by cutting or breaking the sides off the piece and gluing them back on after the windows and gate have been cut. Breaking a piece off is often better than cutting it off. The saw blade takes out some of the wood and when the pieces are glued back together, the terrace will have to be re-cut.

ble so the piece locks into itself. I usually make heart-like shapes that oppose each other. When the piece is cut, push it down until it stops. Turn the pieces upside down and trace along the base with a

Making an Ascending Gate

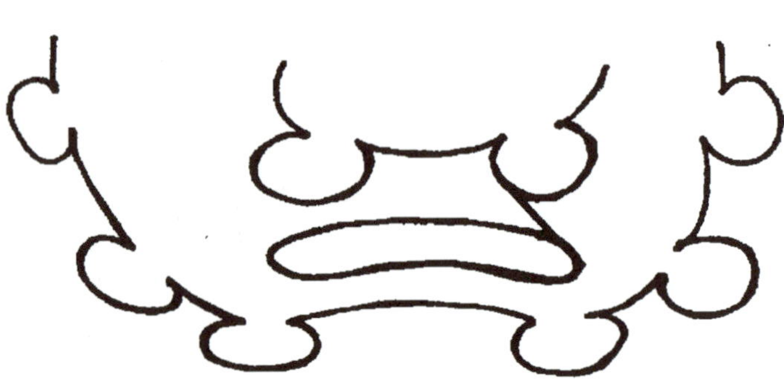

Cut a banana shaped piece directly behind main gate

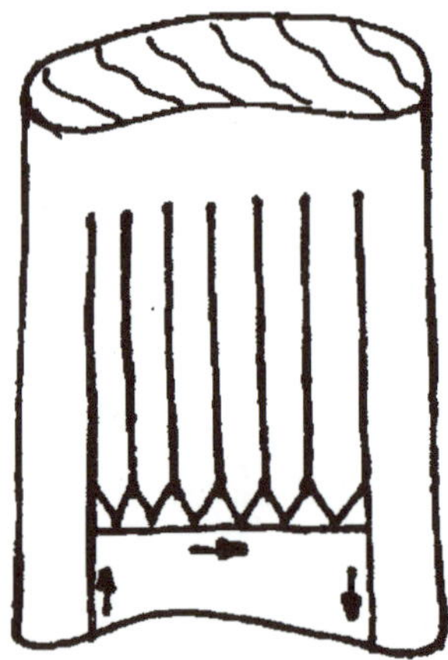

Set the banana piece on its back. Cut out a piece up to threshold level. This piece will later be glued to the underside of the third terrace after the gate has been inserted, to stop it from falling out.

To avoid breaking ,cut the point of the bars first , then cut the bars of the gate. Insert into terrace. Glue removed piece to the third terrace level with the threshold.

Remove the banana piece and place the third terrace on its back. Cut out the gate. Re-insert the banana piece so the base is aligned with the base of the terrace. Mark the outline of the gate with pencil.

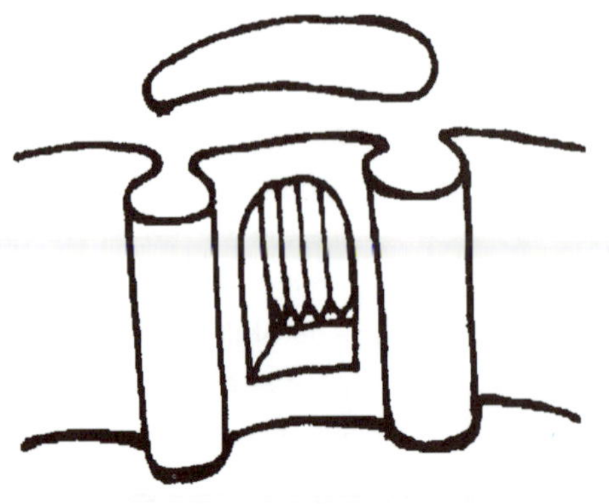

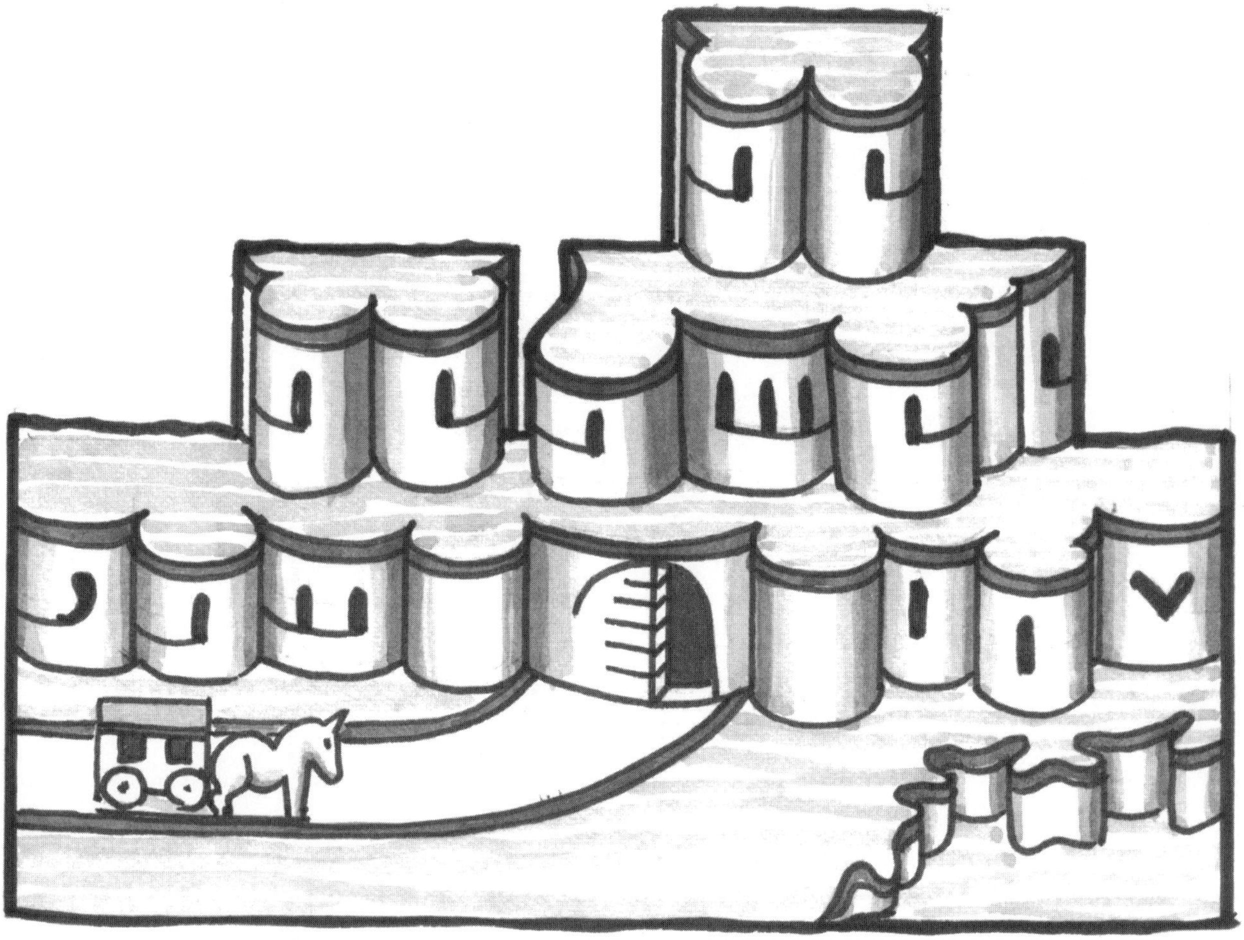

SCROLL SAW CASTLES

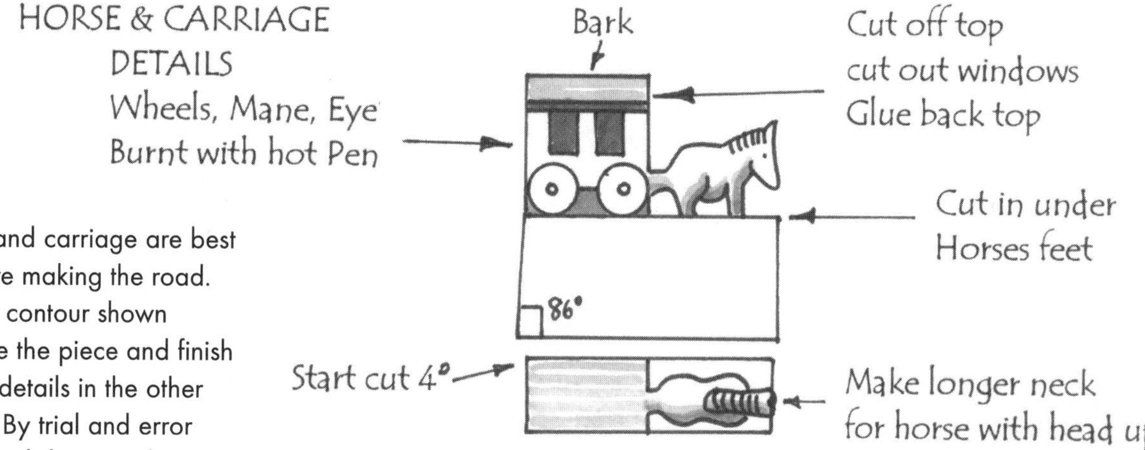

Use interlocking heart-shaped cuts for the cliff face. This piece will move downward to an extended position. Cut away the excess wood protruding from underneath the base of the castle.

HORSE & CARRIAGE
DETAILS
Wheels, Mane, Eye
Burnt with hot Pen

The horse and carriage are best done before making the road. Cut out the contour shown and remove the piece and finish cutting the details in the other dimension. By trial and error sand the road down until it passes just under the feet of the horse.

Cut on one side must be no greater than $3/8$ in. (2 cm) from the back of the castle. This reduces the chance of the castle being back-heavy and toppling over.

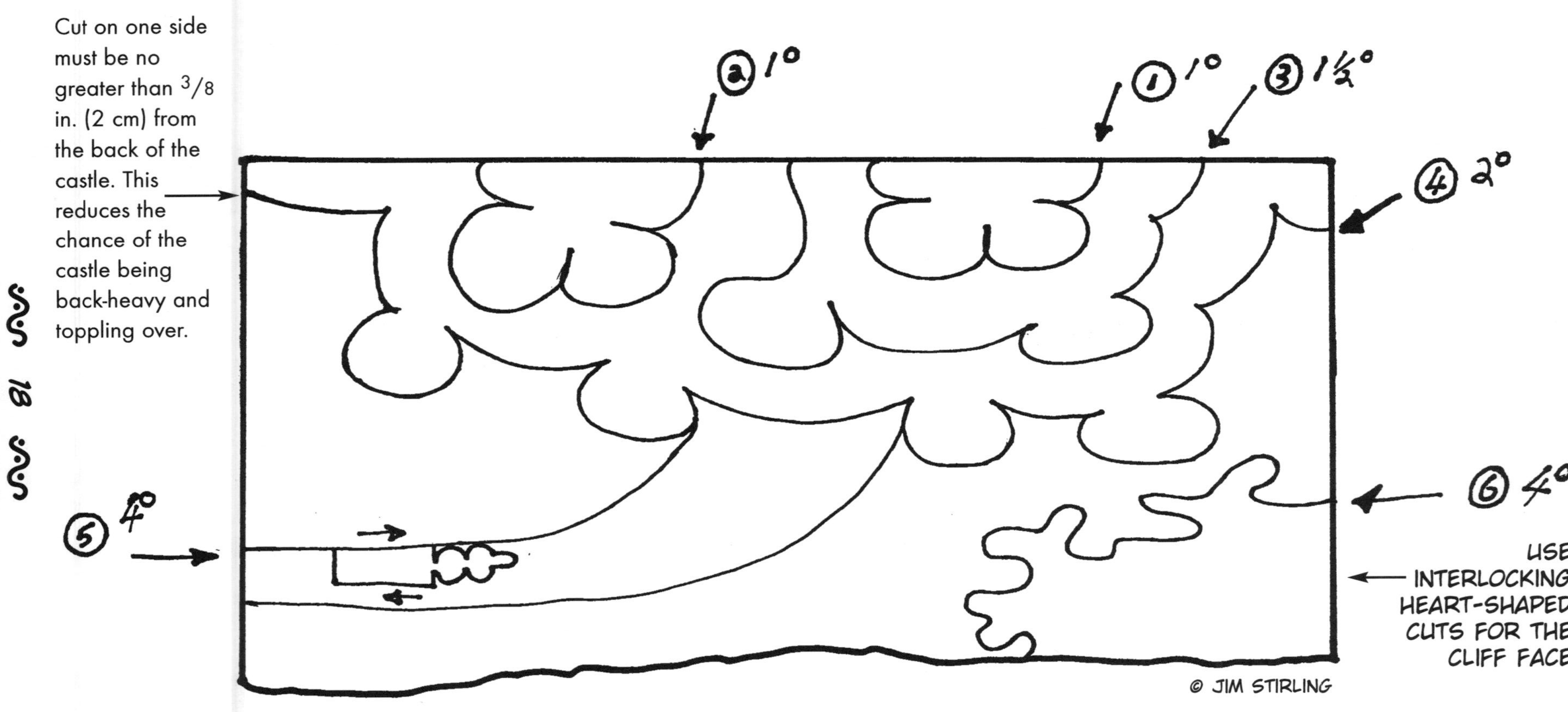

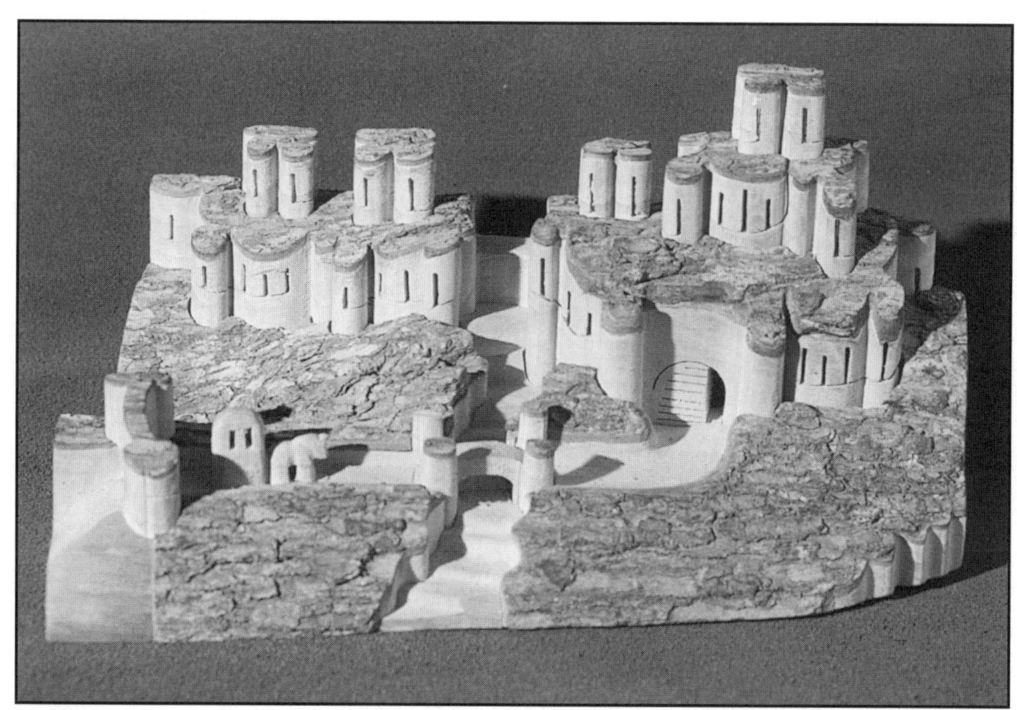

This castle has a waterfall and bridge. It's called "Mother-in-Law's Castle" because the first castle I made like this I gave to my mother-in-law, bless her soul.

MOTHER-IN-LAW CASTLE

This castle demands a piece of wood made from dissecting a fork in the branches. The basic shape needed can be seen from the bird's eye view drawing on page 21. The towers, gates and horse and carriage are similar to those used in the simple castle and the princess castle. On the land formed by the stub of a branch, we have placed an entrance portal. A waterfall tumbles out of the middle of the castle, then forms a cascading river that flows under a bridge and out to an imaginary sea.

The whole castle must literally be cut in half to make the waterfall. Then it is glued back together again. If the river bands have been made irregular, it will make the task of lining up the pieces for gluing much easier.

Follow the order of cutting indicated on the bird's eye view. All is pretty straight forward until you get to cuts 10 and 11. Now start on the cascading river with the pop-up bridge. With the table set at 0 degrees, cut both banks of the river down to where the bridge stands. Starting at the end of one of these cuts, tilt the table to about three or four. Cut in a clockwise direction around the bridge, as shown in the bird's eye view. Take the piece out.

Create the road up through the front watchtower. Cut the road up to the watchtower. Cut the watchtower then cut a portal in the watchtower, level with the road. Alternately, sand the road down so it is level with the threshold of the portal. Adjust the road to go under the feet of the horse.

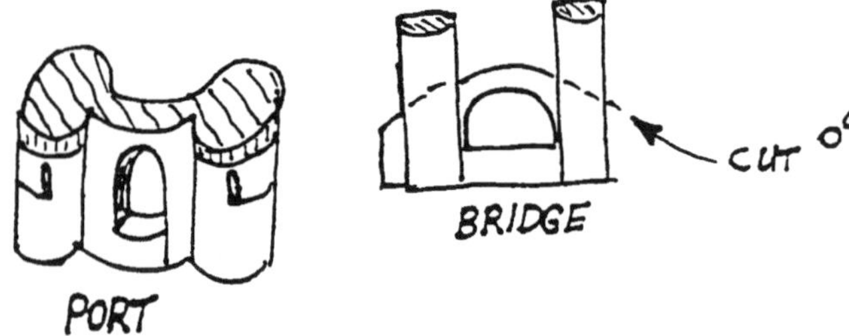

Proceed up to the end of the bridge. It is best to only cut the road down to the level of the bark in this area. Proceed with the road from the other end of the bridge up to the main gate of the castle. Put the bridge piece back in, push it up and mark the ends with your pencil. Remove the bridge piece.

Set the table at zero degrees again. Finish off the river cuts down to the front of the wood. The castle will now be in two halves, plus the two parts that will be the waterfall and cascades.

Set the bridge piece aside to be dealt with later. Take the back waterfall piece and cut a concave piece of the back about 3/4 inch thick. This will form the waterfall between the two outer terraces of the castle. Place this piece on its side and cut the bark off. Glue this piece and the two outer terraces together.

Now concentrate on the cascading river. Lay the pieces on their sides. Starting at the thickest part, cut a cascading river, just below the bark level. Glue the two parts of the river to the two parts of the land in front of the castle. If the banks of the river are cut crooked, it will be easier to line the pieces up for gluing. Wood glue is the best, but it takes time to set. If you're impatient, like me, you can use hot glue.

When the glue has set, place the bridge back in its area. Because some wood was lost when cutting and gluing the river, the bridge will be tight on the ends. Release the saw blade from its top bracket and insert it from underneath, up between the side of the bridge and the higher part of the river. With the table at 4 degrees, cut around in a clockwise direction to widen the cut again. Do this carefully, until the bridge comes up to where it was before

the gluing. Remove the blade. Push the bridge up and mark where the river meets the bridge.

Place the bridge on its side. With the table at 0 degrees, start in from one of the ends. Proceed at road level in a smooth outward bow, through the towers, down to the mark on the other end of the bridge. Set the top piece to one side.

Take the base piece and cut in from the bottom, on the inside of the pylons. Proceed up in a bow, parallel to the top of the bridge and down the inside of the other pylon. Then cut across again along the mark you made to represent the water level of the river. Set this piece to one side.

Set the top piece on its base and carefully cut off the pylons on the bridge. You may need to sand these pylons round before gluing them back on the base of the bridge.

Take the base piece and cut in from the bottom, on the inside of the pylons. Proceed in a bow, parallel to the top of the bridge and down the inside of the next pylon. Then cut across along the mark you have made to represent the level of the water. Place the main castle and front together. It will be a bit tight around the area of the waterfall. Recut this area as described for the bridge.

Now put the whole piece back together and see how it looks. Is it suitable to give to a mother-in-law?

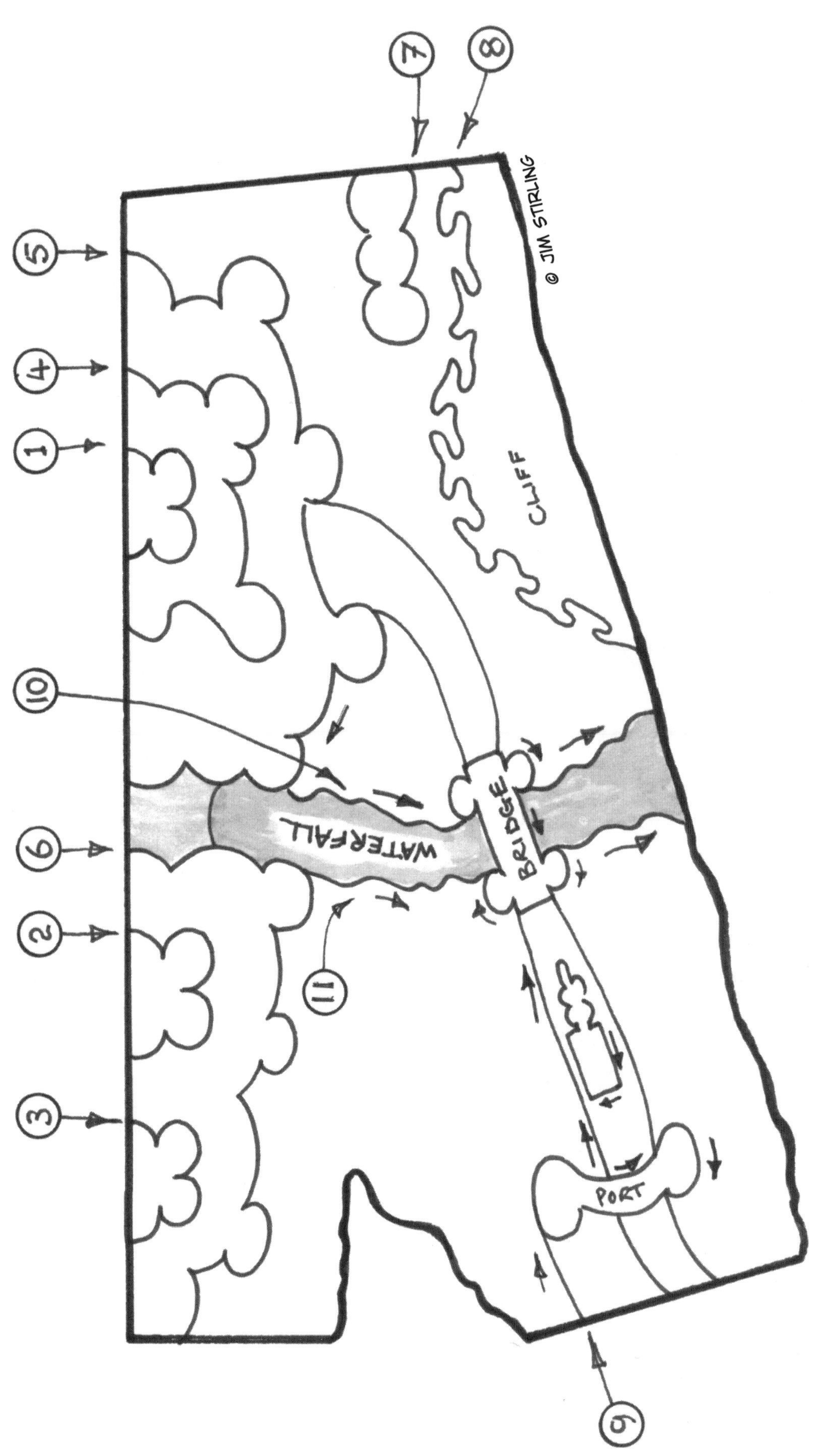

© JIM STIRLING
CLIFF
WATERFALL
BRIDGE
PORT

③ LAY THE SAWN OFF TOP WITH BARK UP.
CUT OFF THE CORNER POSTS.
GLUE BACK ONTO BRIDGE LATER.

② ROAD LEVEL. LAY BRIDGE ON IT'S SIDE.
CUT A NEAT BOW.
DISECTION CORNER POSTS TO ROAD LEVEL.

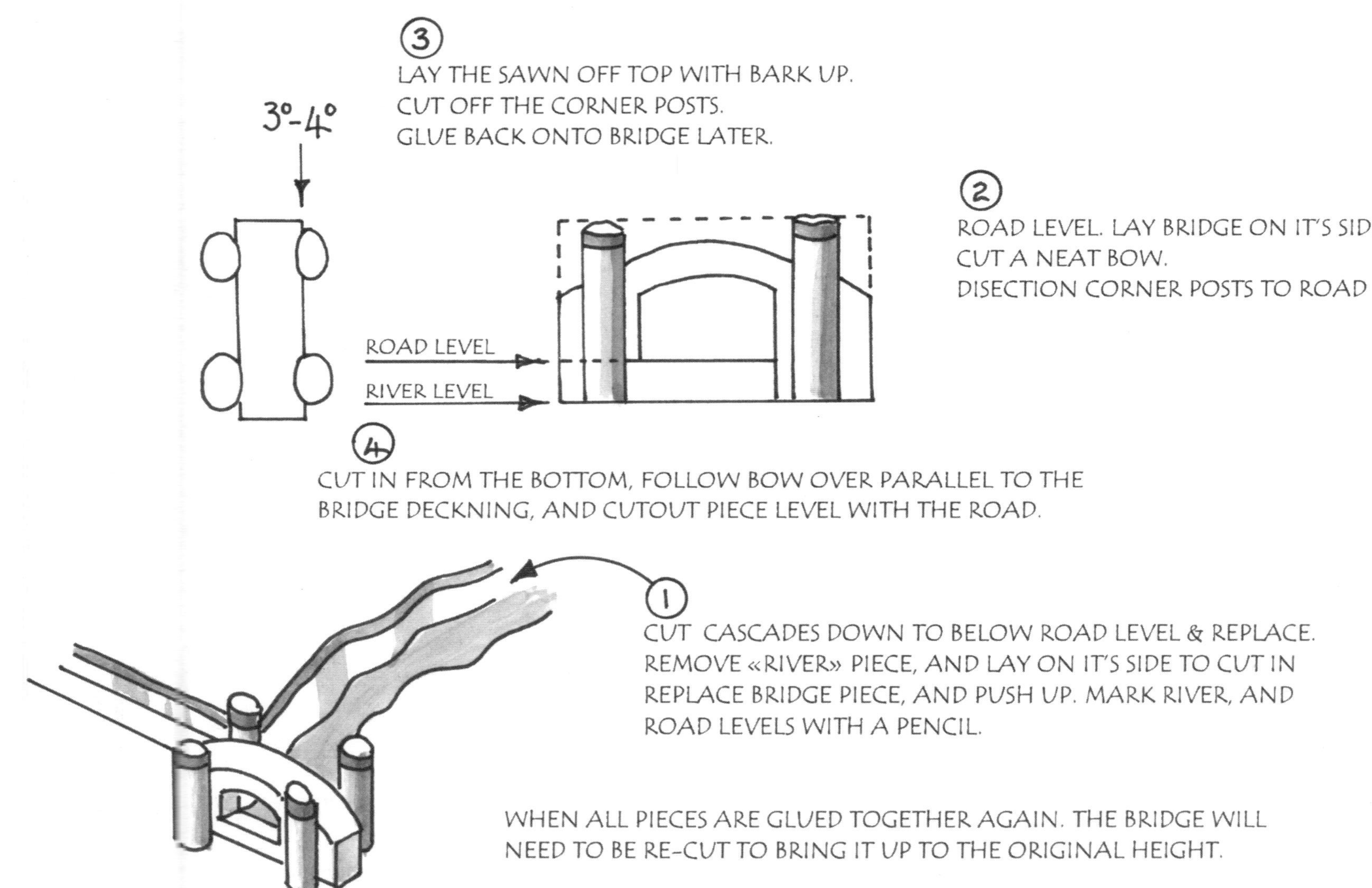

④ CUT IN FROM THE BOTTOM, FOLLOW BOW OVER PARALLEL TO THE
BRIDGE DECKNING, AND CUTOUT PIECE LEVEL WITH THE ROAD.

① CUT CASCADES DOWN TO BELOW ROAD LEVEL & REPLACE.
REMOVE «RIVER» PIECE, AND LAY ON IT'S SIDE TO CUT IN
REPLACE BRIDGE PIECE, AND PUSH UP. MARK RIVER, AND
ROAD LEVELS WITH A PENCIL.

WHEN ALL PIECES ARE GLUED TOGETHER AGAIN. THE BRIDGE WILL
NEED TO BE RE-CUT TO BRING IT UP TO THE ORIGINAL HEIGHT.

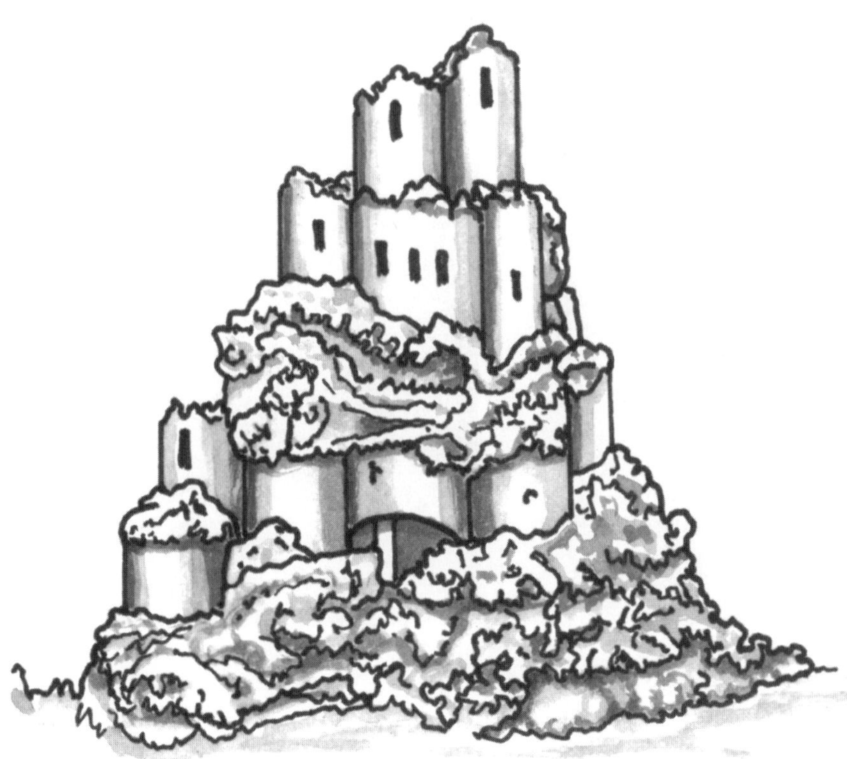

No two burl castles are ever the same. While challenging to cut, these castles are often very dramatic when completed.

BURL CASTLES

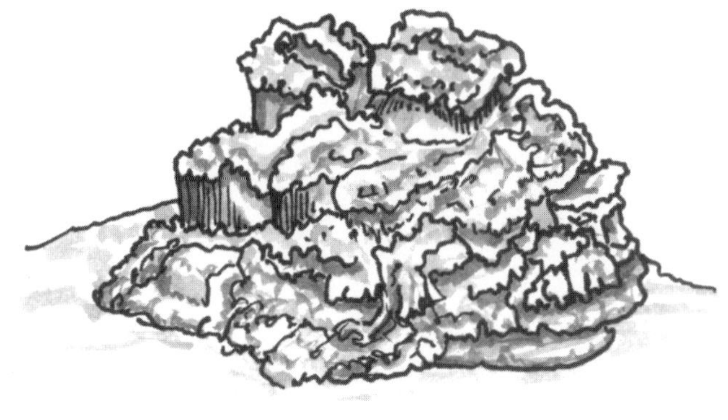

I can't make any drawings of these kinds of castles because no two pieces are alike. Some pictures of pieces can be found on the covers of this book and in the gallery section. Use these photos to give you an idea of what burl castles look like. You'll get more ideas as you look at specific burls.

Cut the burl down to a height that will go under the saw blade. You can choose to leave the piece in its original rounded form, or you may choose to cut the back off. Windows are easier to cut in on a flat-backed castle. I use a branding iron to burn in the windows on pieces that I want to leave rounded. I shape the tip of the soldering iron by grinding the tip into a long window shape, flat across the bottom and rounded on the top.

Before cutting the levels, decide which side of the burl will be most suitable for the front. Make use of humps and subtleties in the wood by making your cuts so that these will be accentuated.

If the piece is rounded, the first tower must be cut a fair way into the middle of the wood; otherwise this tower will be too low. Make sure when cutting the rest of the towers that they start close to the back of the wood. This will keep the piece from toppling over backwards.

If you find that the piece topples, you can fix it in one

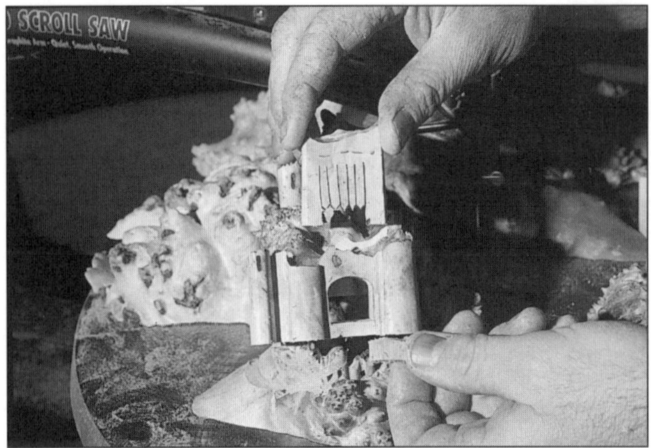

The removed front terrace shows an ascending gate.

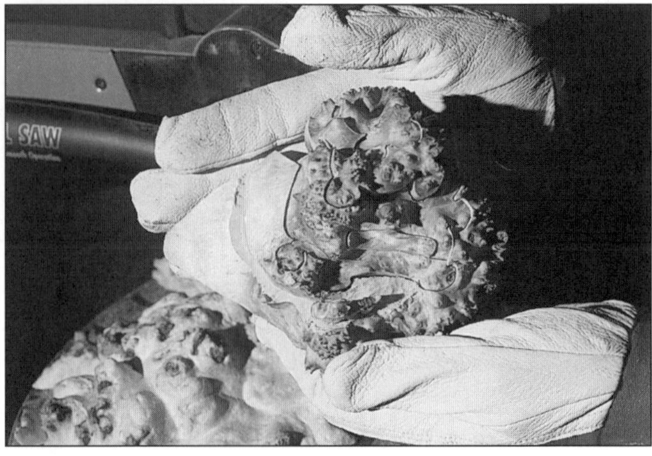

A bird's eye view of a collapsed burl castle. Note the gloves. Gloves help to protect your hands from the burl's spikes.

of two ways. Try sanding the bottom on a belt sander so that the whole castle leans a little forward. Otherwise, you can cut a piece of plywood in the shape of the base. Put the castle together and glue the most forward piece to the plywood base. The pieces, although moveable, will not be able to be removed.

Make a horse and carriage coming up the road if space allows. You can be very creative with the road up the slope at the front of the castle. The terrain might call for a hairpin bend or a tunnel. If there is a valley or a chasm to cross, you can create a bridge out of other material and glue it in place. Experiment with sunken inner courtyards as well. If you want to sink a piece down, cut counter-clock-

wise with the right side of the table tilted down. Often the wood in burls is not as stable, and although these faults can create character, they can also create problems by breaking away.

If I make a castle that I really like, I burn my wife's or daughter's name on the bottom of it straight away. Otherwise I may end up selling it or giving it away. Castles made from burl pieces are so original that you may never get another one like it again.

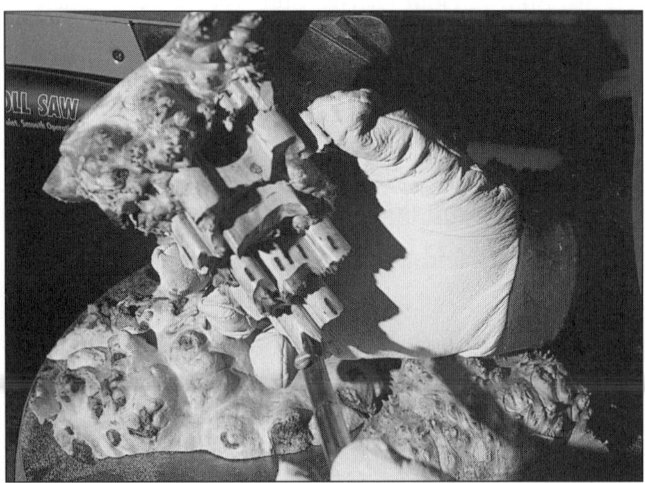

Burning the windows on the tower with a branding iron.

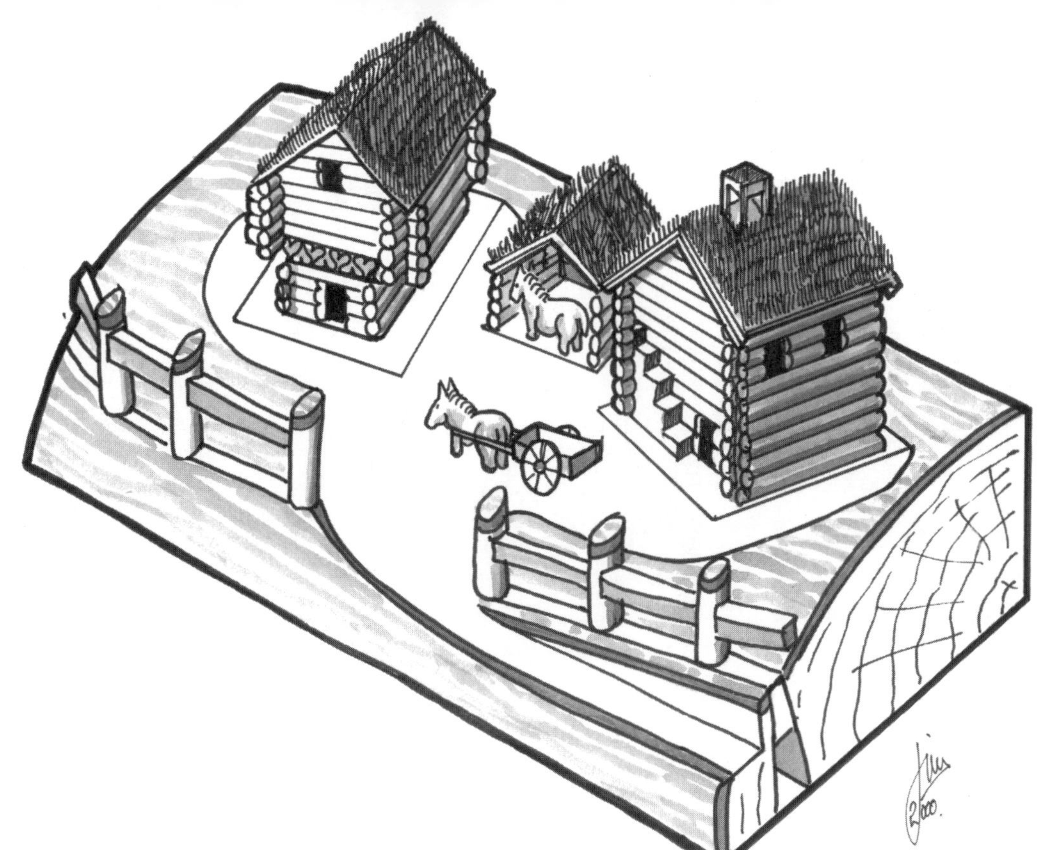

The same techniques used
to create castles can also
be used to create scenes.
This is a scene typical of
the Norwegian countryside.

NORWEGIAN STABBUR

This project focuses on making buildings in a scene rather than single castles. All of the pieces, however, are based on the same methods. Each is conical and wedges either up or down into position to create a multi-level scene. Scenes from where I have lived and traveled have influenced the works you see in this book. Movies and comic books have also given me ideas. Some sections of the drawings are very detailed, such as the roof tiles. Often, in the real model, the bark left on the top of the piece is enough to suggest a roof.

Stabbur: On older Norwegian farms there was always a "stabbur," or food storage house. Often the stabbur had stone steps separate from the bottom story. Many buildings had sod roofs. Putting a goat up on the roof provided grass cutting services. Illustrations to guide you in cutting this piece are shown on page 28.

With the table set at about one degree, cut out a fairly large square. Cutting the building on an angle to the back of the wood seems to give it more perspective. Remove the piece. With a Dremel tool, cut away the bark in the front of the building. Insert the piece again, push it up and mark along the front of the building. Lay the piece on its back. Cut angles off each side to form the roof. Leave some of the bark for effect. (See the illustration on page 28.)

Cut a roof off the piece by cutting a little lower down and parallel to the top.

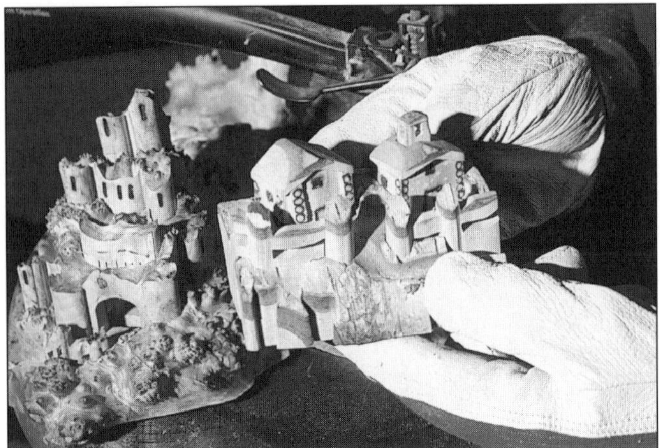

The completed Norwegian farm scene.

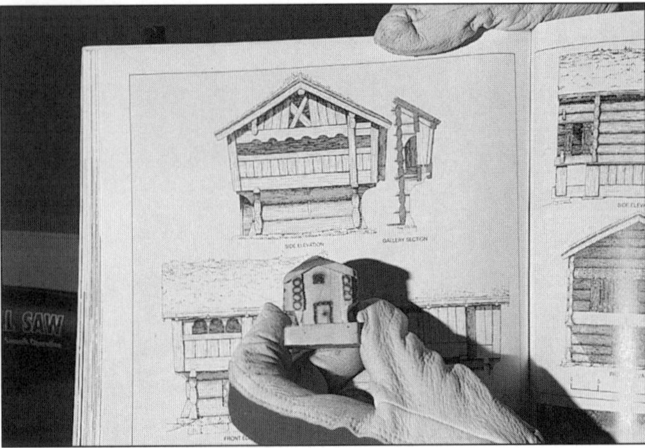

A picture of a stabbur as compared to the model built for this scene.

Put this roof to one side. Cut the base off the piece along the marked line. Insert the base again and mark right around the wall of the host piece.

Mark the top of the building as shown in the illustration on page 28. This will make the impression of layered logs on the outside of the building. The inner square will form the lower story. This piece must be inversely conical. Set the angle at about four degrees. Cut in from the back in a counter-clockwise direction. Exit backward through the insert cut. Extend the story down to its limit. Glue it to the base, then glue the roof on the building. Use a burning tool to detail the ends of wooden logs at each corner.

Because the piece extends up farther than it would if it were a single piece, the walls of the upper story will rub against the narrowing walls of the host timber. This can be rectified by sanding the roof and walls back. You can also place the table at about three to four degrees and cut in a clockwise fashion around the three side walls of the host piece. Be careful not to let the saw cut below the mark line indicating the height of the base.

Bell house: Another building on a Norwegian farm is the barn that houses the bell. Illustrations to guide you in this piece are found on page 29.

Set the table at one degree. Cut into the center from the back of the building and cut out a small

square in a clockwise direction. Remove the piece and lay it on its side. Cut angles on four sides in the bark to form the roof of the bell tower. Cut the roof off just below the wood level. Cut out notches from two sides so that pillars are left at each corner of the building.

Now glue the roof back on. Cut the roof angles on the building. Insert the bell tower. If you are really keen, you can turn a miniature bell on a lathe and glue it in the bell tower. Decorate this building to resemble logs.

Post and rail fences: Set the table at about two or three degrees. Saw in from the sides of the piece in a clockwise direction. Make straight cuts for the rails followed by round cuts for the posts. Proceed to within 3/4 in. (2 cm) of the middle. Make an end post and come back along the fence in the other direction, finishing off the back sides of the rails and posts. Do the same on the other side of the wood. Leave some place between the middle posts to allow a road to come through, up to the building. Push the fences up and mark along the bark line of the host piece.

Remove the pieces. Cut down from the top beside a post and across at the bark/wood level to form the top of the rail and up the next post. Cut in from the bottom, up beside the posts along the bottom of the rail, down the next post, back along the ground line and out the insert cut. Leave the bark on the tops of the posts for impression.

Finishing touches: Often it is easier to cut and make the buildings and fences to the height required, then when finished, adjust the amount of extension. For fences, the bark in front can be sanded down until the fence is showing at the right height. Add a horse and buggy on the road, if you wish. Consider cutting out some horses and cows in areas available for such pieces.

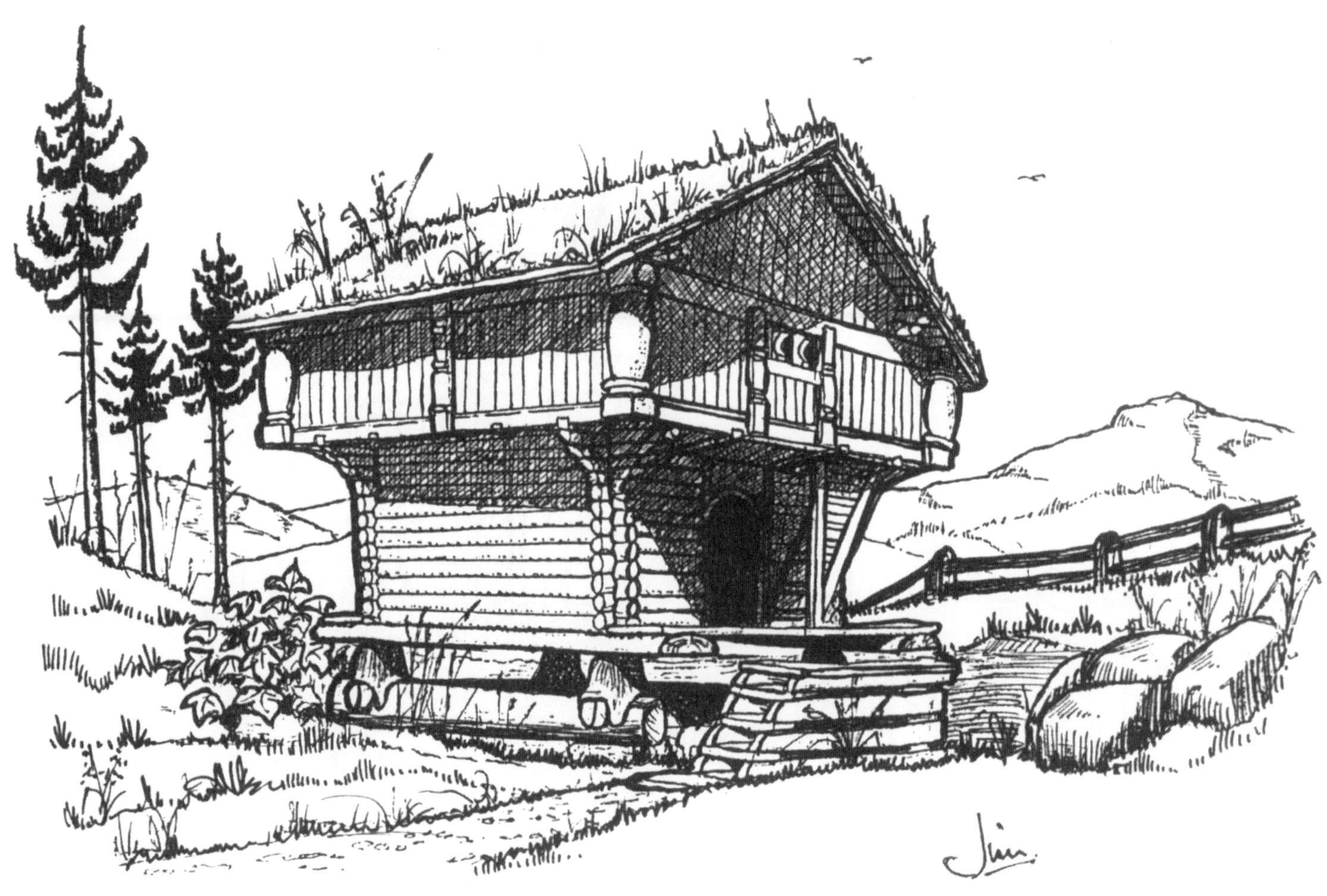

NORWEGIAN
STABBUR

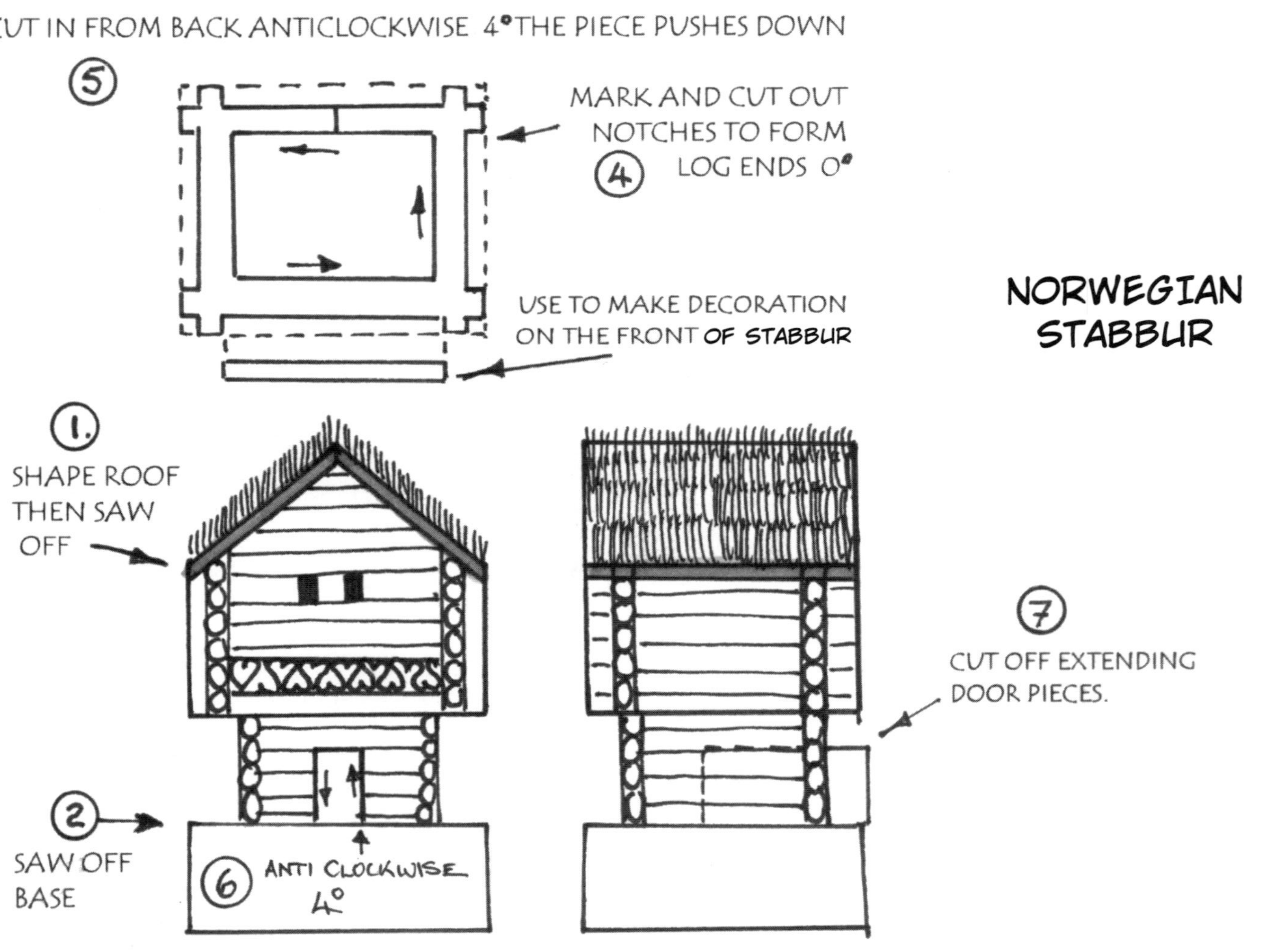

NORWEGIAN BELL HOUSE

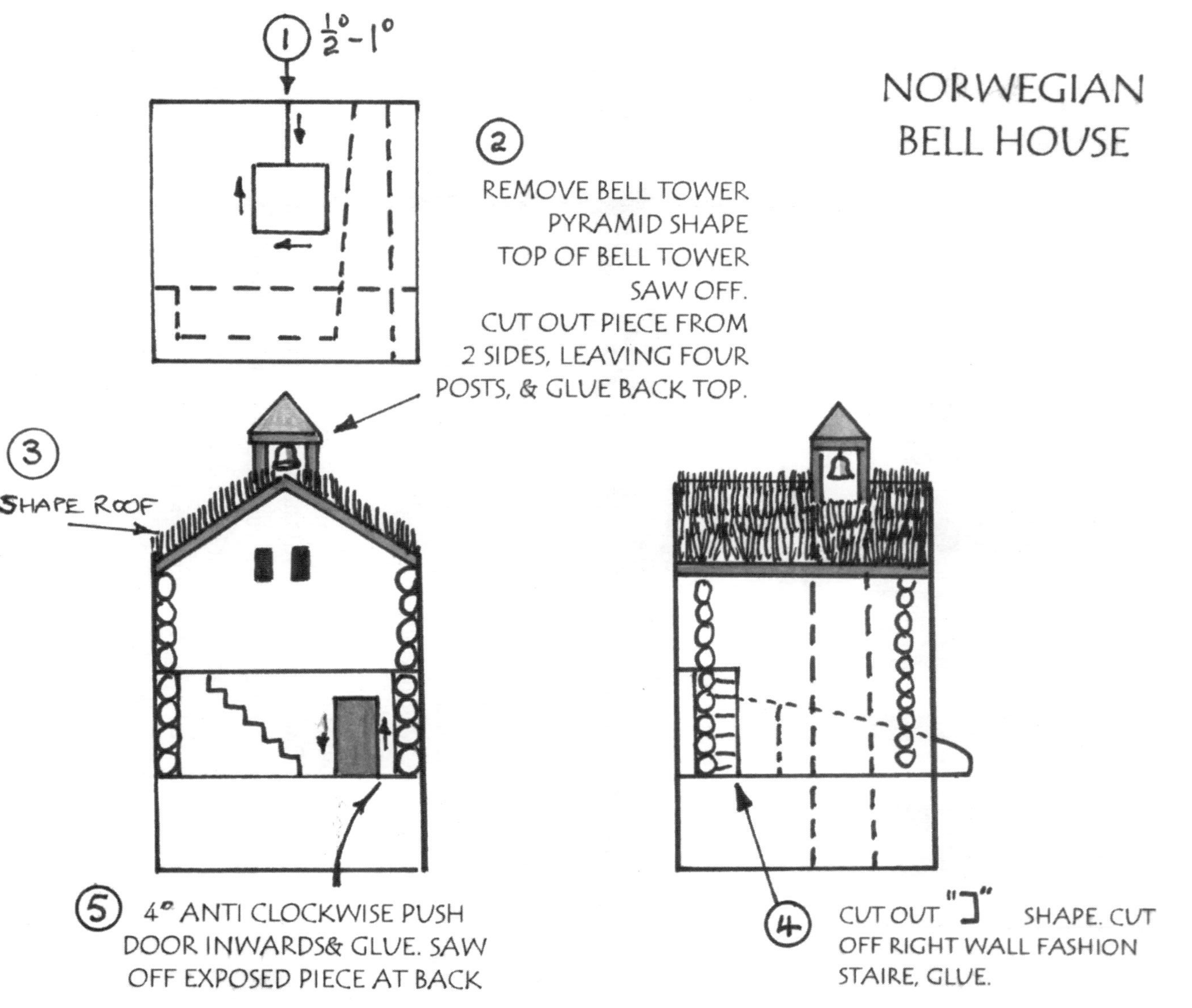

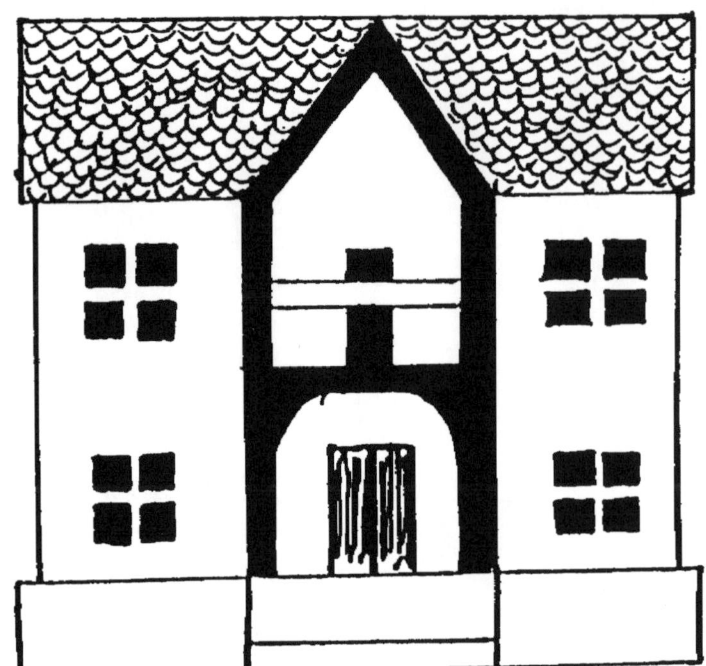

Add a main house to the
previous project to create a
large Norwegian farm
scene.

NORWAY FARM HOUSE

This larger farm scene has all the elements of the Norwegian stabbur, but with an additional, central accommodation house. The style in the illustration above is very typical of a Norwegian main house. Cut out the main building as in the drawings on the following pages. The main house has two stories and an entrance verandah.

Cutting tips: Cut out the building as shown in the bird's eye view. Remove the piece. To help shape the roof, the verandah and roof must be sawn out of the main building. Set the saw at three degrees. Come in from the left side of the verandah. Proceed into the middle of the main building, along the eaves and back out the other side of the verandah. The piece will push up slightly. Shape the roof with a superfile or on the saw. Cut off the roof, then cut the building off the base. Cut back the front and sides of the building so that the roof has a natural overhang. Next, cut the verandah away from the front wall of the building and cut a door in the wall section.

Cut the verandah as shown. It may be easier to put a finer blade in the saw to do this job. Cut into a piece of plywood and leave it in place around the blade. This will make the fine sawing more stable. Be careful not to break the thin wooden posts. Adjust the railings if they are too intricate. The main posts and floor are most important. Glue the roof, base and verandah back in place. Burn in the windows.

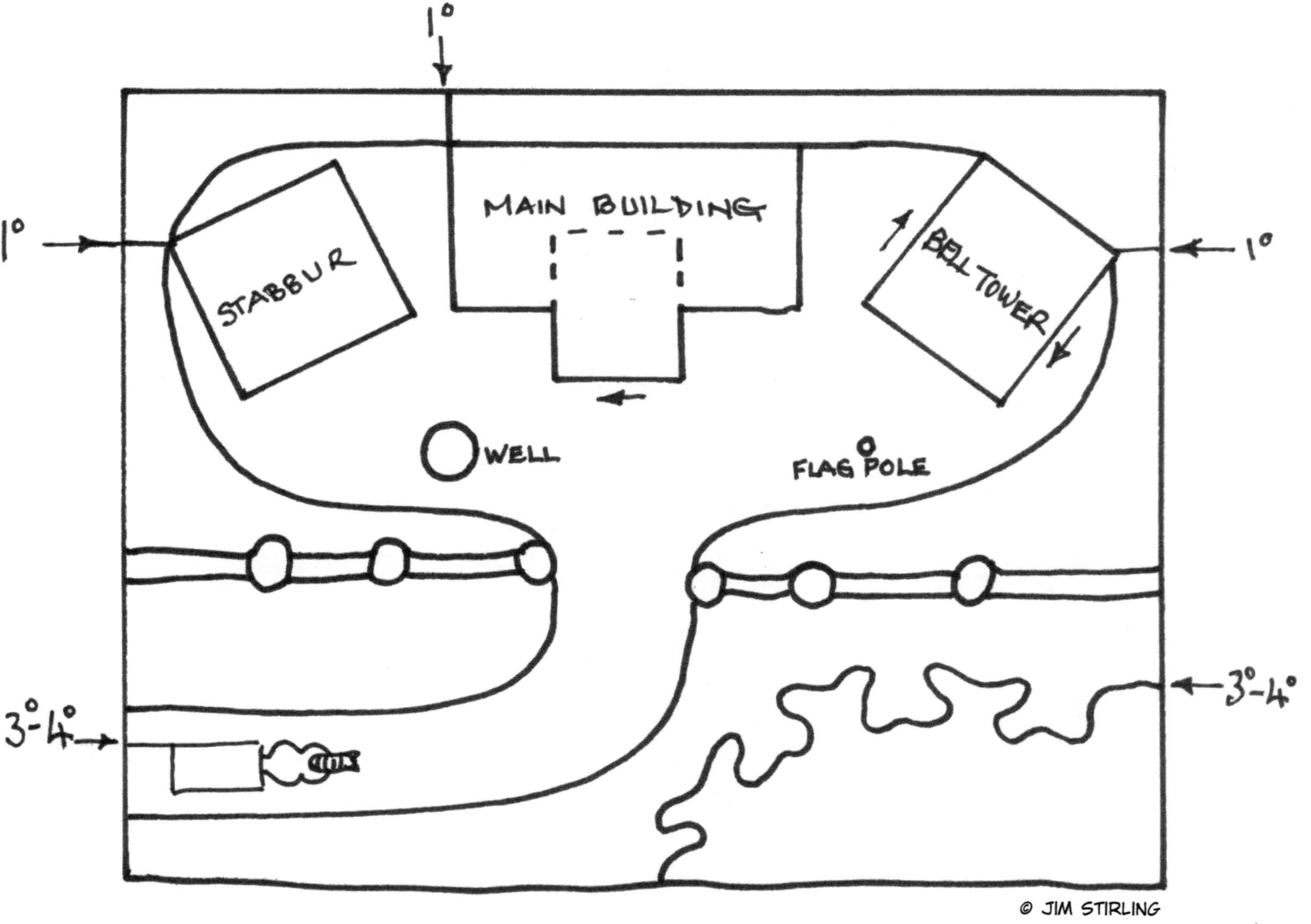

MAIN BUILDING
STABBUR
BELL TOWER
WELL
FLAG POLE
1°
1°
1°
3°-4°
3°-4°
© JIM STIRLING

NORWEGIAN FARM HOUSE

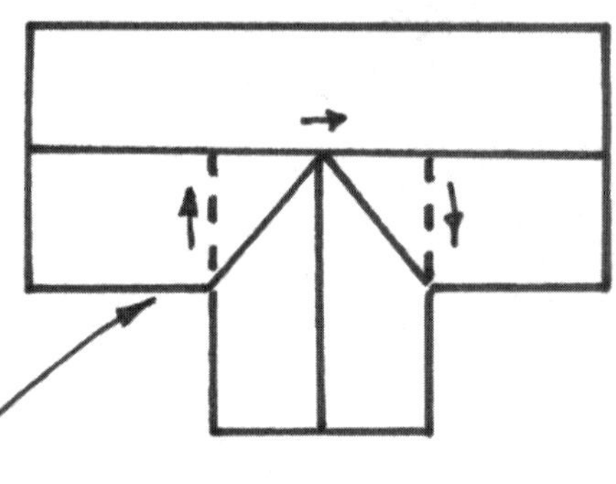

SHAPE MAIN ROOF
WITH A SUPER FILE
CUT OFF ROOF.

3' – 4' CUT OUT
VERANDAH
PIECE SLIDES
SLIGHTLY
UPWARDS.
SHAPE ROOF
TO SUIT THE
MAIN BUILDING.
CUT OFF ROOF
SAW OFF
VERANDAH
LEVEL WITH
FRONT OF
HOUSE.

CAREFULLY FORM THE **VERANDAH**
AS **SHOWN IN BLACK. THE RAILINGS MAY**
BE TOO FINICKY
A FINER BLADE
& A THIN PIECE
OF PLYWOOD
AROUND THE
BLADE MAY
MAKE IT EASIER.

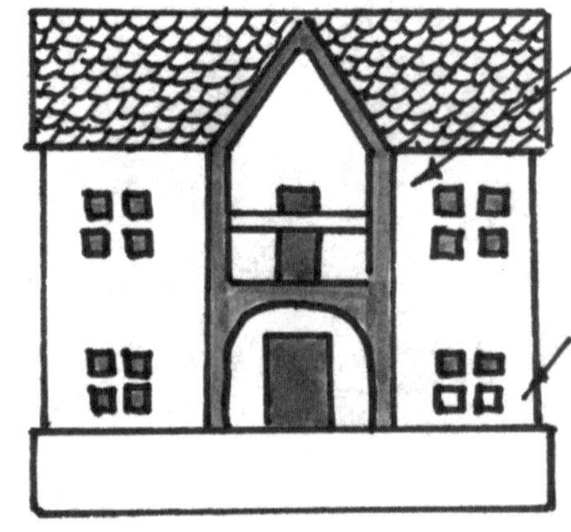

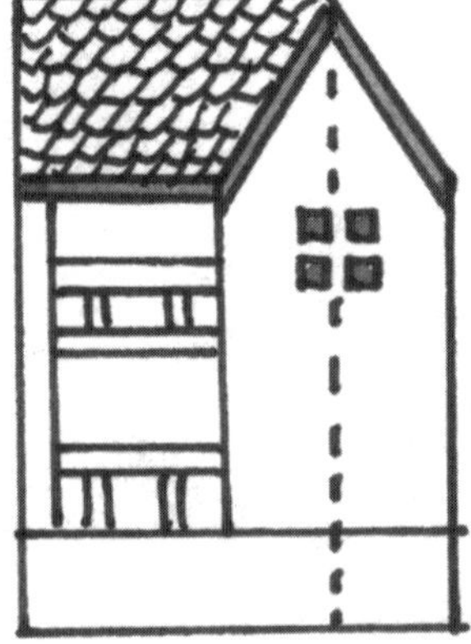

CUT BUILDING
OFF THE BASE
THIN DOWN
WALLS ON THE
MAIN BUILDING
CUT OUT DOOR
GLUE EVERYTHING
BACK TOGETHER.

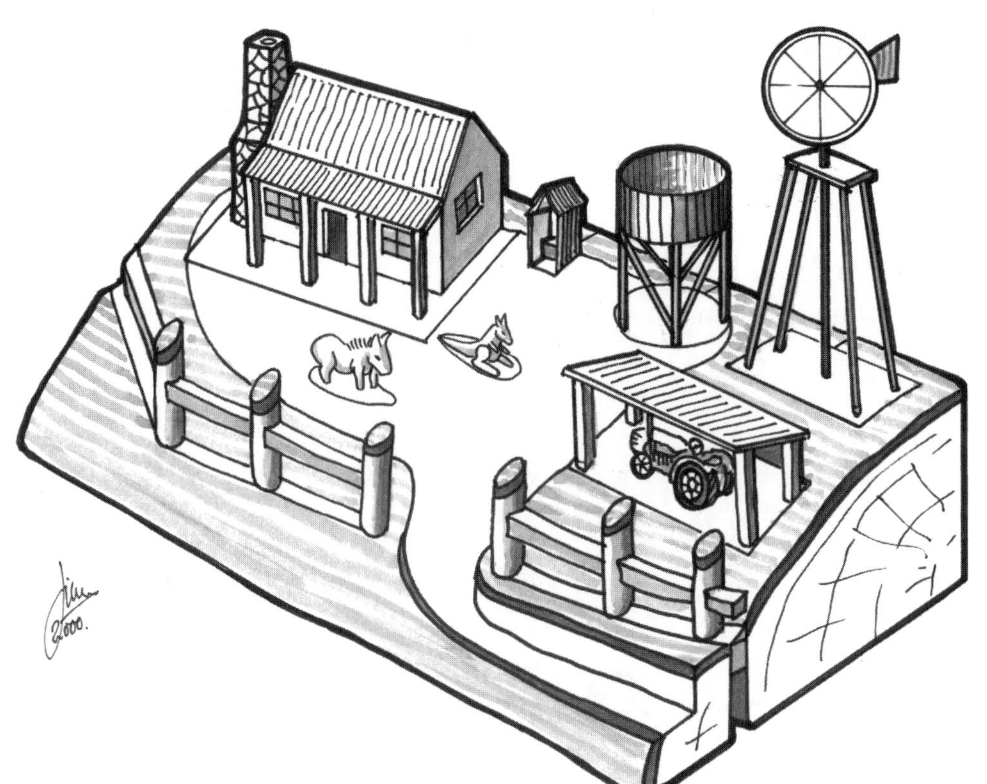

This farm has all the accessories: a windmill, a watertower, a kangaroo, and last but not least, a dinkum dunny—or an outhouse as our American mates would call it.

AUSSY FARM

Main building: Cut out the main hut as shown in the diagram. Remove the piece. Cut off the chimney. Stand the hut on its side. Form the roof of hut and verandah. Cut off the verandah, then cut evenly spaced poles as in the diagram. Cut a door in the main building and brand in the windows. Glue the verandah and the chimney back on.

Stable: Cut out the rectangular building. Form a flat roof with drainage to the back. Cut the roof off. Cut a horse shape, front or side on. Remove the piece. Cut the building off its base. Cut the middle out of the building, leaving two sides and a back wall. Push the horse piece up into the base. Mark where it comes through and finish off the horse with hooves standing on this level. You could also make a tractor as shown in the drawing. Glue the walls to the base and the roof to the walls.

Windmill and watertower: Make the tank round but with a small lug at the back. This will stop the piece from rotating in the hole. A slight rotation will effect the amount of elevation the piece will have. Cut the lump off down to ground level, then cut the windmill as in the diagram. Use toothpicks to elevate the pieces.

Dunny: This is just a small, square building. Out in the bush, dunnies rarely have doors. Lay the piece on its back and cut the roof. Lay it on its side and cut out the walls leaving the back wall. Take this small piece and cut out the front door. Glue the walls back in place. You may even make a miniature throne by boring a hole in a piece of wood and cutting around it.

    Finishing touches: Cut the fences as described in the Norwegian Farm Scene. Follow the diagram to make the kangaroo.

POST & RAIL FENCE

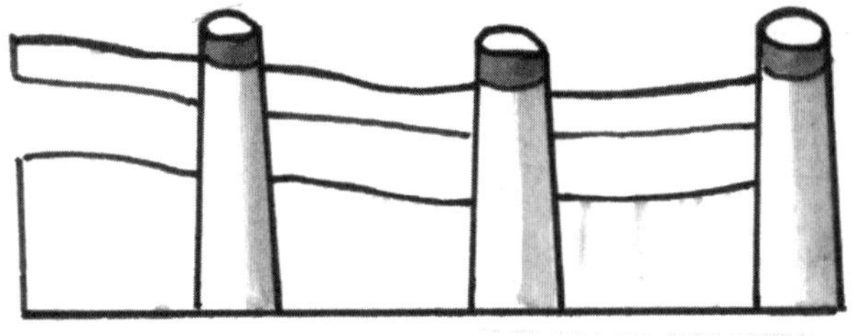

SAW ENTRY POINT.   O′   CUT OUT
SPACE BETWEEN RAILS AND
GROUND LEVEL.

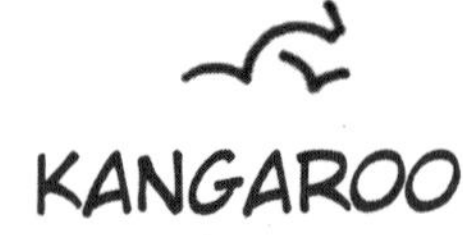

KANGAROO

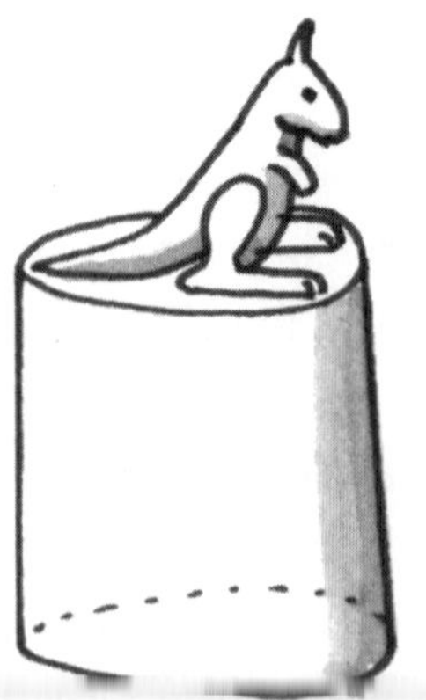

EARLY AUSTRALIAN
DWELLINGS

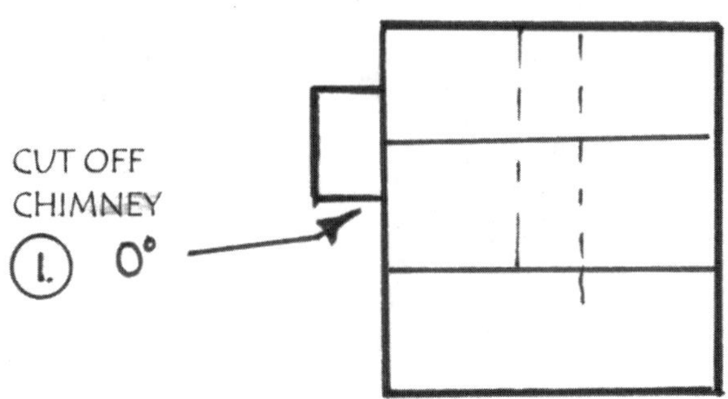

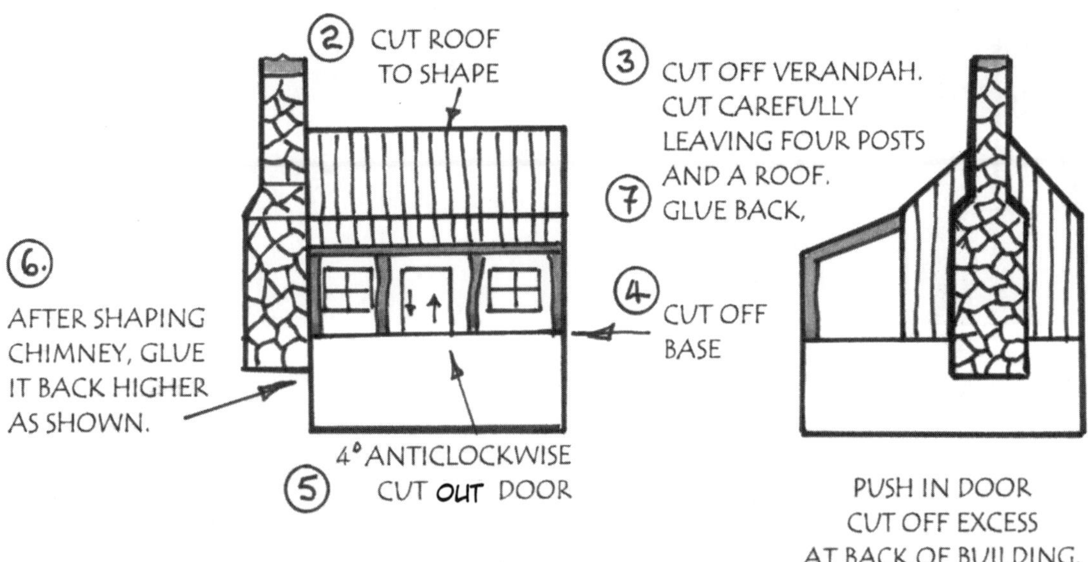

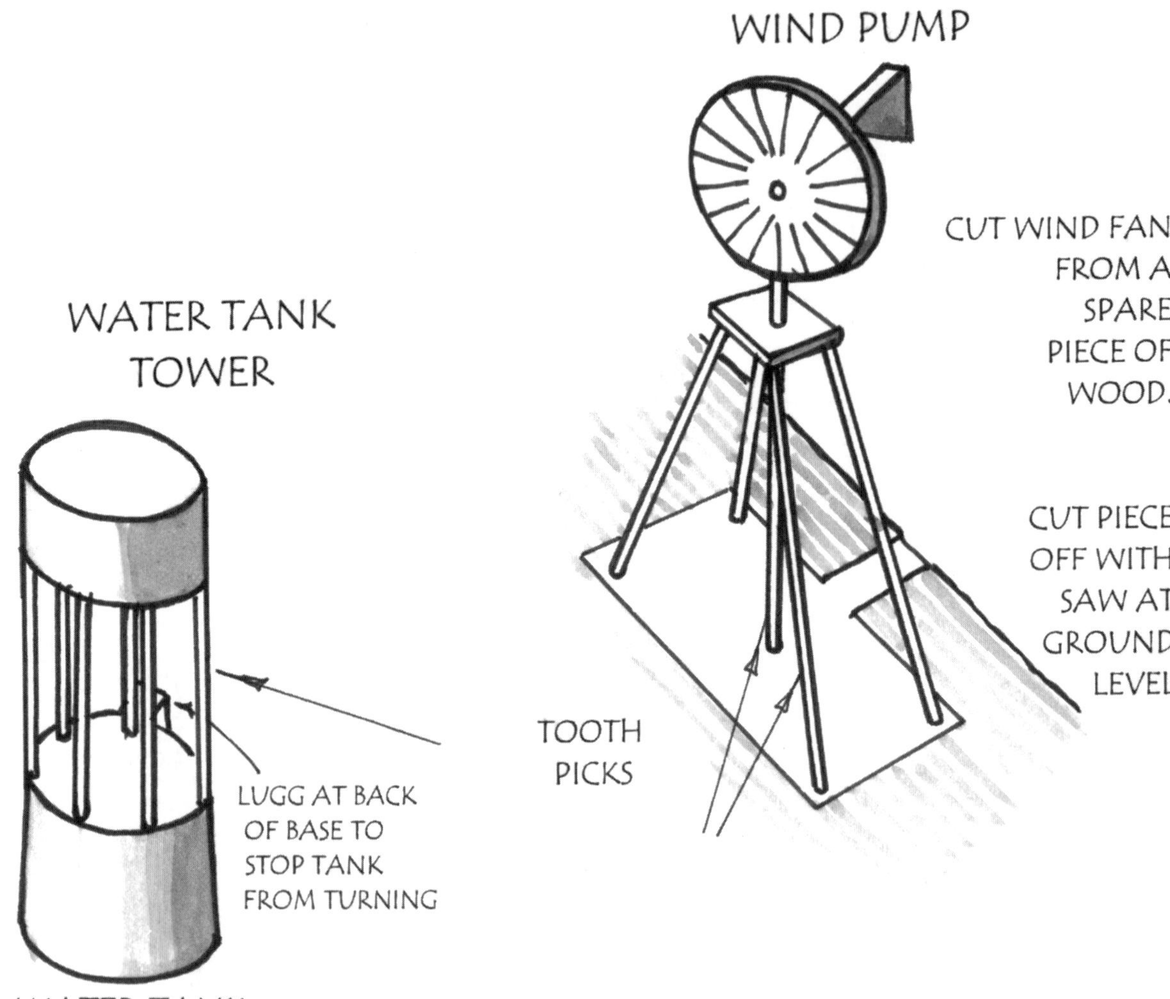

WIND PUMP
WATER TANK
TOWER
CUT WIND FAN
FROM A
SPARE
PIECE OF
WOOD.
CUT PIECE
OFF WITH
SAW AT
GROUND
LEVEL
TOOTH
PICKS
LUGG AT BACK
OF BASE TO
STOP TANK
FROM TURNING
WATER TANK

② MAKE TRACTOR
SHAPE 3° REMOVE

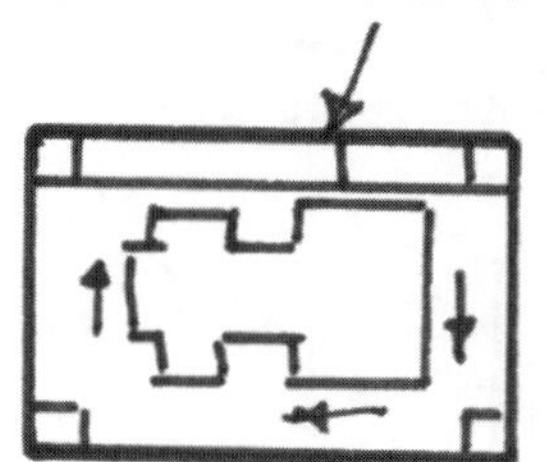

TRACTOR
SHED

① SLOPE ROOF
AND CUT OFF

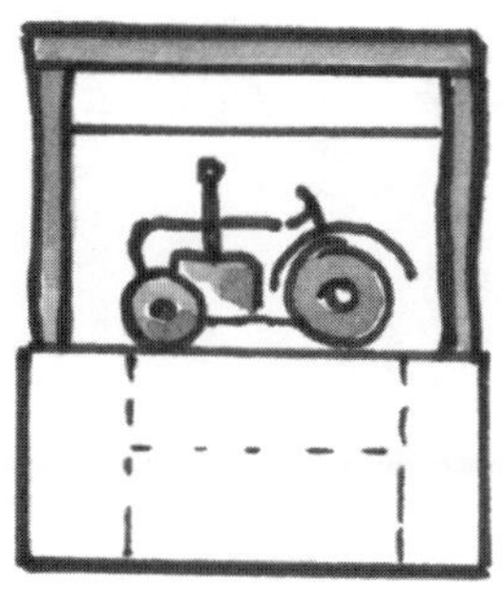

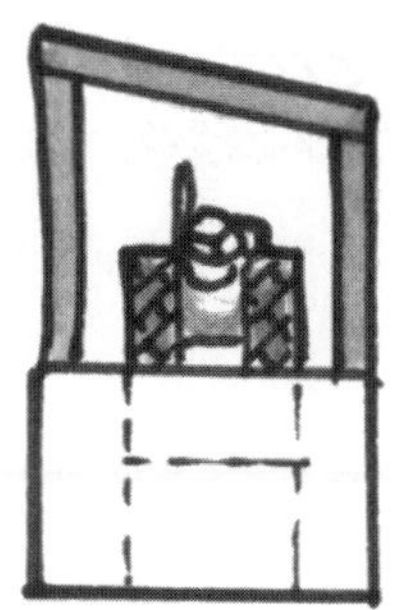

③ CUT OFF BASE CUT OFF BACK WALL
FORM FRONT POSTS

GLUE WALL & POSTS ON BASE – ROOF

④ SHAPE TRACTOR & BURN IN
WHEEL DETAILS ETC.

DINKUM AUSSI. DUNNY.

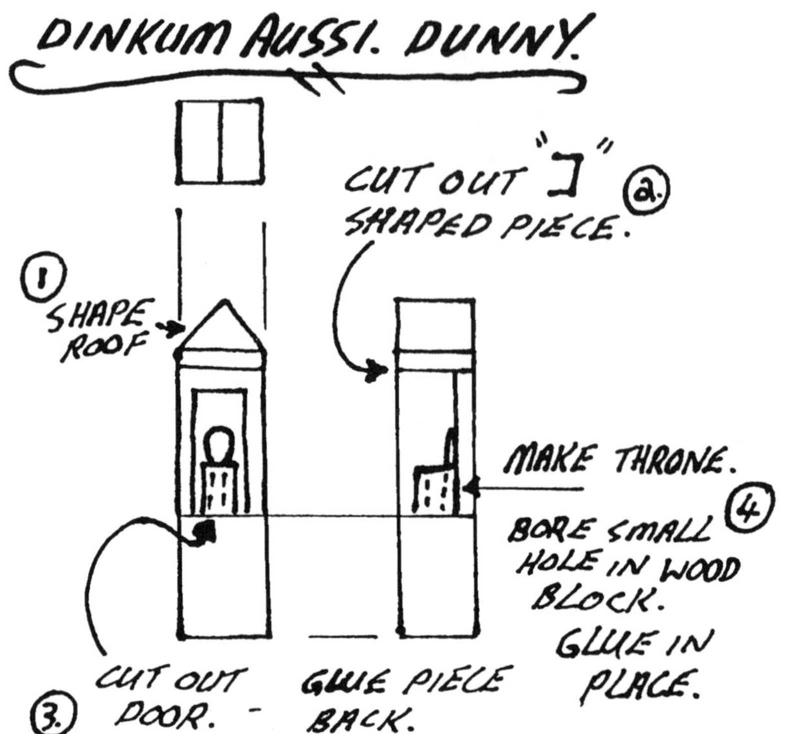

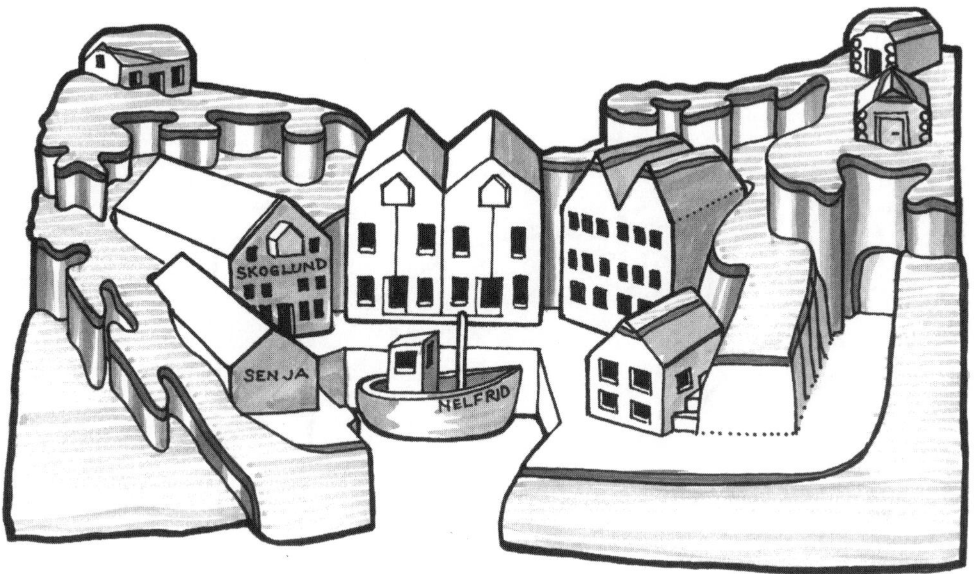

I met my wife in northern Norway at a place called Narvik. Adjacent to Narvik is the Lofoton peninsula. Fishing is the main income here and the fjords are dotted with small fishing villages.

NORWEGIAN FISHING VILLAGE

This is a rather advanced project that requires a bit of concentration to get the angles right. In the bird's eye view, note the order of cutting.

Harbor: First cut out the harbor at zero degrees. Remove the piece. Set the saw to four degrees and cut out the docks in a counter-clockwise fashion. This will make the piece extend downward. Mark the extent of the protrusion. Remove this piece and lay the piece on its back. Cut off the protrusion. This cut will leave about a 3/4 in. (2 cm) high, "C"-shaped piece at the bottom to form the boardwalk or docks. Set the piece to the side.

With the saw on the same angle, cut out the individual buildings. It is best to proceed from the left-hand side in a clockwise direction, making a square or rectangular building behind each angle of the dock. At the back end of the dock, leave a space between the buildings. This will allow the dockside to be stabilized by the host piece when it is glued in place again.

Cliffs: Set the table at about 1/2 degree and cut the cliffs. The cliff on the right side is started on the side of the piece. Make the cut as tortuous as possible to give

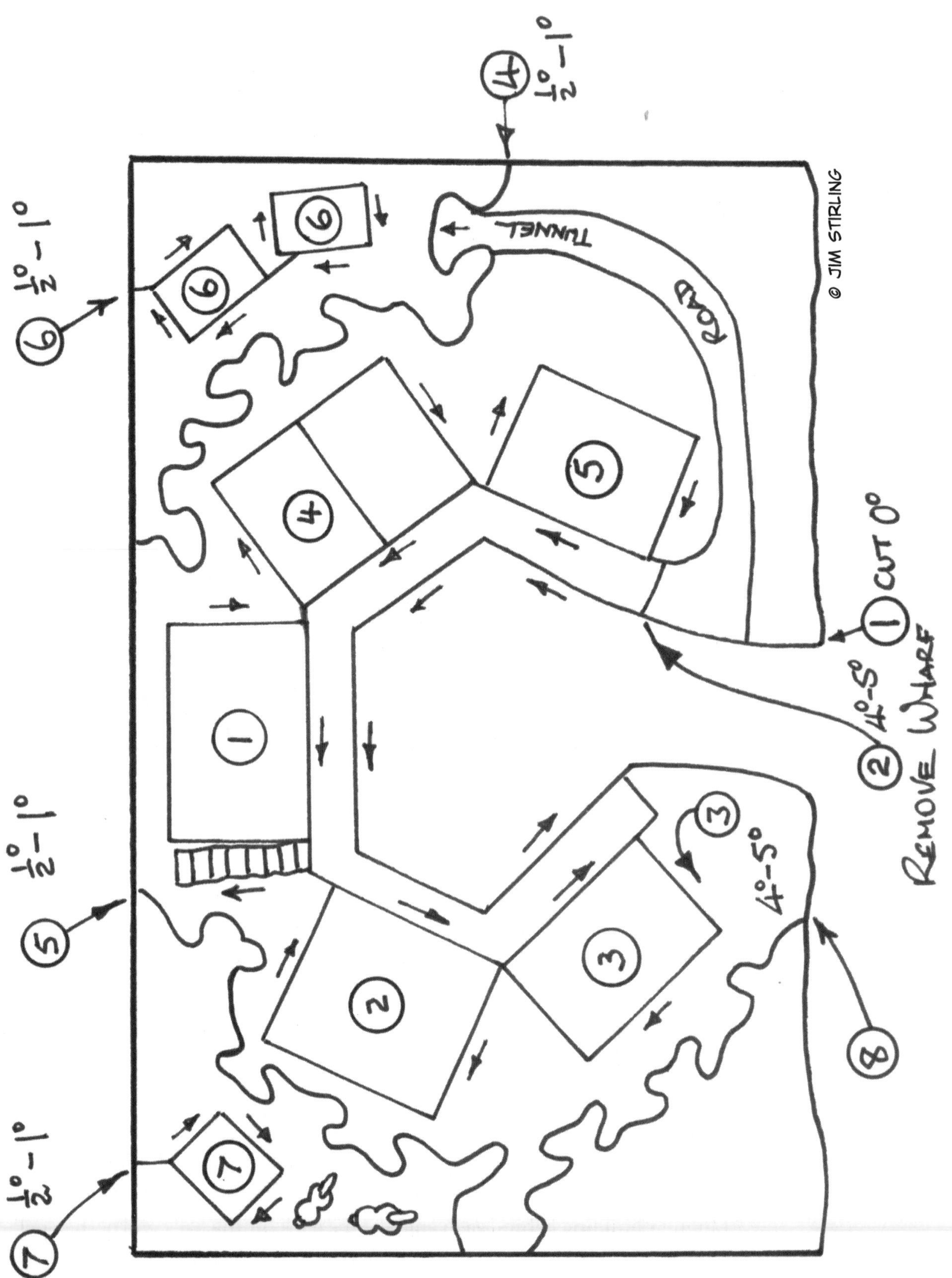

TUNNEL
ROAD
© JIM STIRLING
CUT 0°
REMOVE WHARF
4°-5°
4°-5°

the impression of ruggedness and also to lock the pieces together. I use open heart shapes opposing each other. Cut along the area directly behind the building, being careful not to come too close. Cuts that are too close will weaken the timber. The cut for the cliff on the left is started at the back of the piece. It exits out the side.

To cut the cliff at the front of the piece, set the table at about five degrees. Proceed from the side if making a forward cliff on the right-hand side. Start the cut in the front and proceed to the side if the cliff is on the left-hand side. Push the piece down, mark the amount of protrusion, and cut off the excess.

Buildings: Remove the high cliff pieces and cut the individual mountain farm buildings into these pieces. You can add a stabbur and a horse or simple dwellings suitable to life in the high hills. Lay the cliff on its back cut a tunnel entrance about half way up the cliff.

Glue the wharf back in place. Insert all the buildings and push them up tight. Mark where the fronts of the buildings meet the wharf. Cut the buildings as suggested in the diagrams. Some buildings have a winch house protruding from the top story. The winch was used to move fish and other goods into the warehouse or factory. To create a winch house, set the table at zero degrees. Lay the piece on its back and cut the roof to shape. Cut in from the side along the line of the wharf height. Cut out the door. Tilt the table to four degrees. Cut the shape shown in the diagram in a clockwise direction.

One of the buildings at the back has a staircase leading up to the mountains behind. Cut down from the top beside the building to the wharf height. Break the piece off, fashion steps on the saw, then glue the piece back on.

Boats: The boats in this scene are made separately. Norwegian boats of this type are usually small, stable craft that ply the rough Northern Sea. Cut the horizontal profile of the boat and wheelhouse first, then cut off the wheelhouse. Turn the boat on its base and cut its vertical profile. Use a

Dremel tool to form the keel of the boat. You can also carefully make the deck of the boat, leaving a narrow railing around the edge. Cut the wheelhouse down to fit within the railings on the deck. Glue the wheelhouse in place. Drill a small hole vertically through the deck and insert a round toothpick for the mast. Burn a suitable name on the bow of the boat. Burn in wheelhouse windows with a square branding iron.

Finishing touches: Use a square window-shaped branding iron to decorate the buildings. With a fine-tipped burning pen set on moderate heat, write in the names of suitable notables that could live in this town and own the businesses or have boats named after them. Cut a road from the dockside to the tunnel with a Dremel tool. Also cut down the cliffs that protrude out between the buildings. You can also cut out a motor car shape in the road area, before making the road.

NORWEGIAN FISHING BOAT

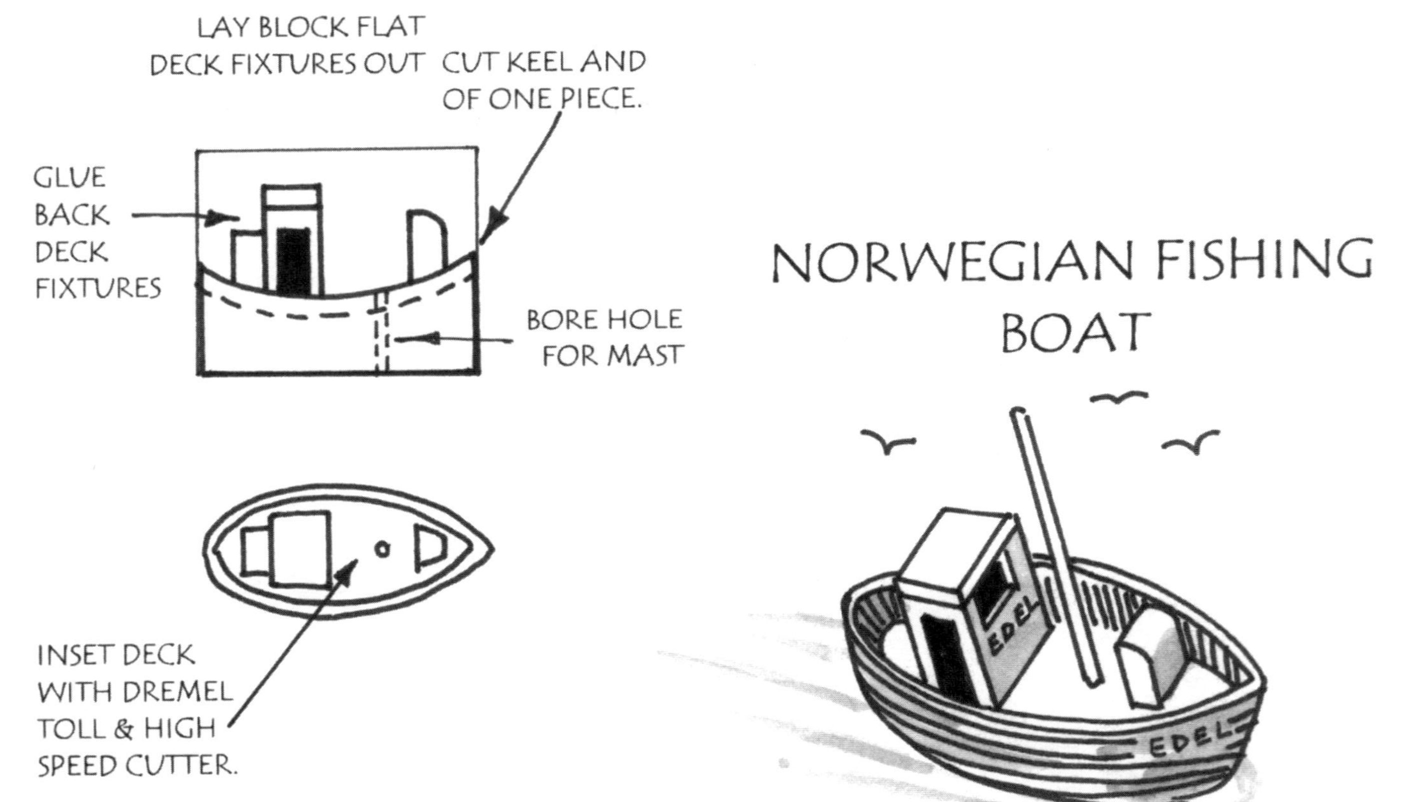

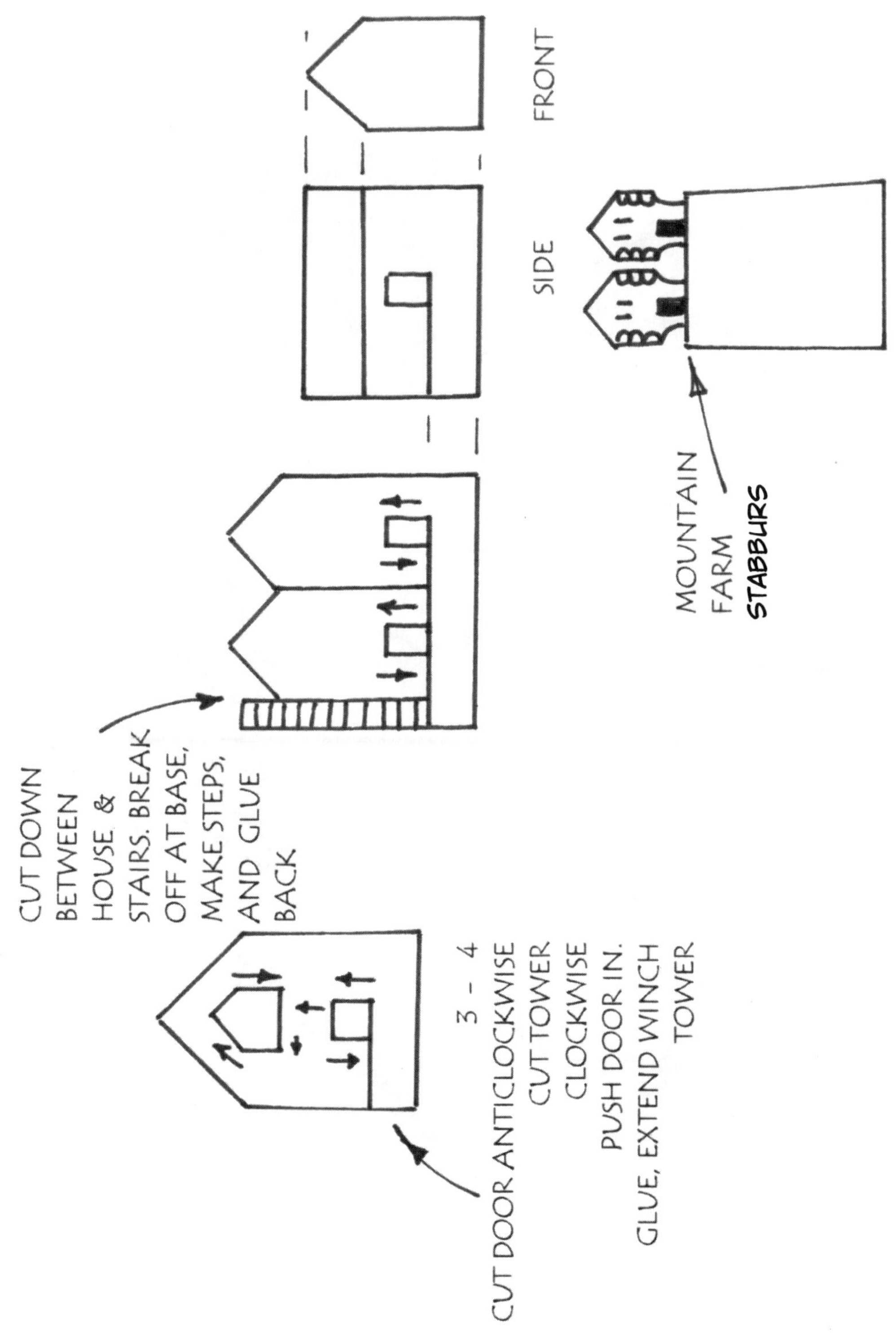

FRONT
SIDE
CUT DOWN
BETWEEN
HOUSE &
STAIRS. BREAK
OFF AT BASE,
MAKE STEPS,
AND GLUE
BACK
3 - 4
CUT DOOR ANTICLOCKWISE
CUT TOWER
CLOCKWISE
PUSH DOOR IN.
GLUE, EXTEND WINCH
TOWER
MOUNTAIN
FARM
STABBURS

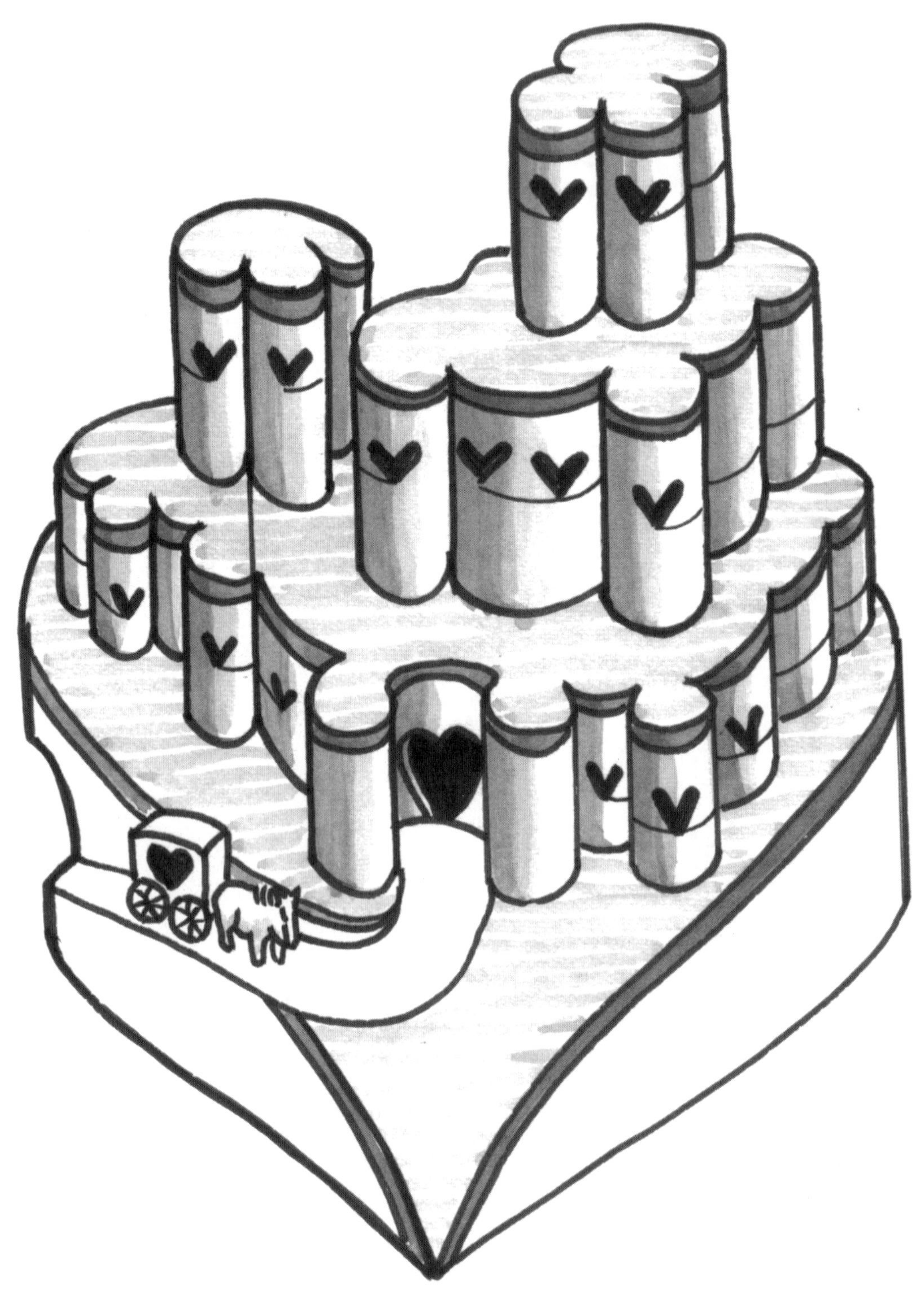

Scroll Saw Castles

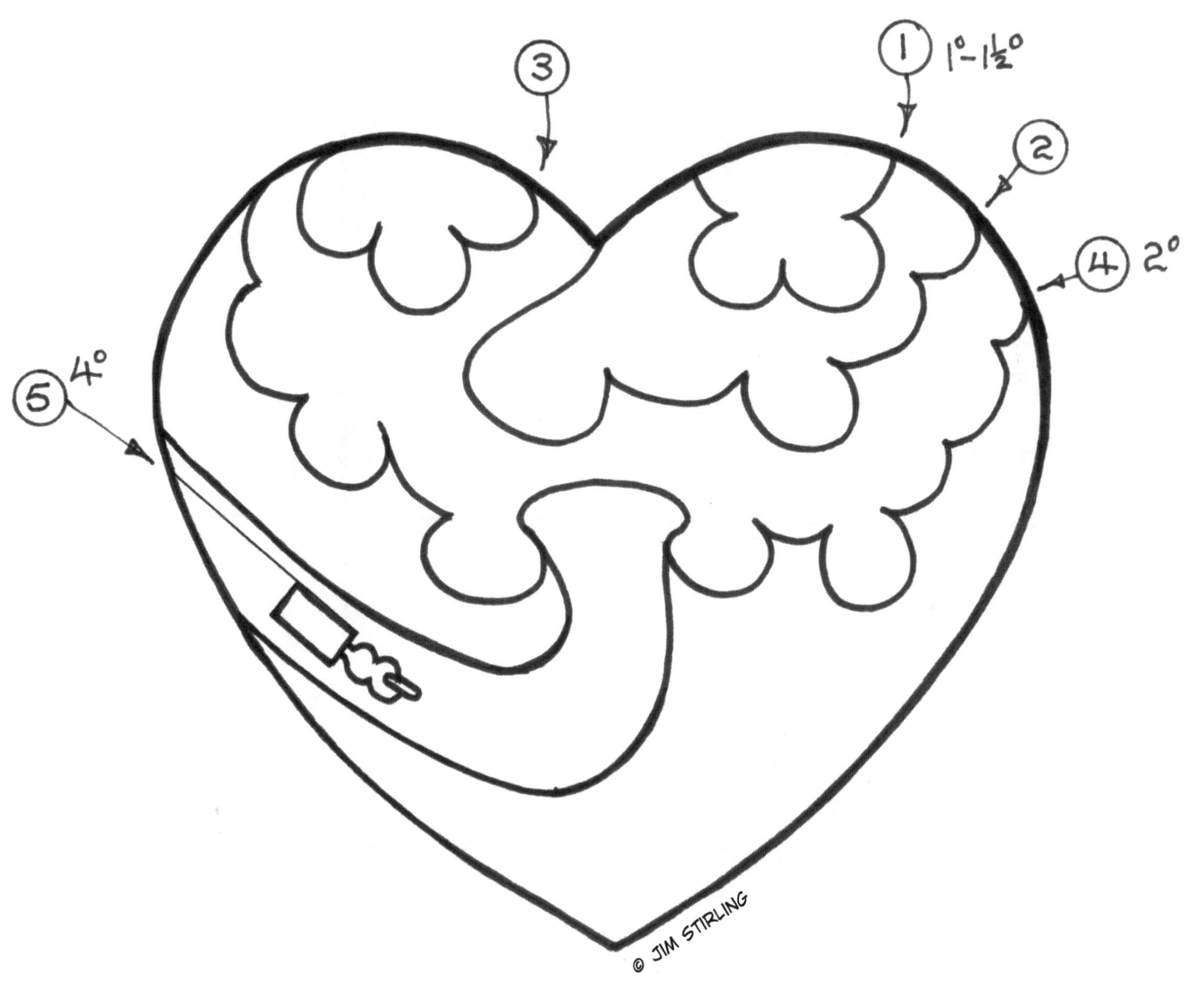

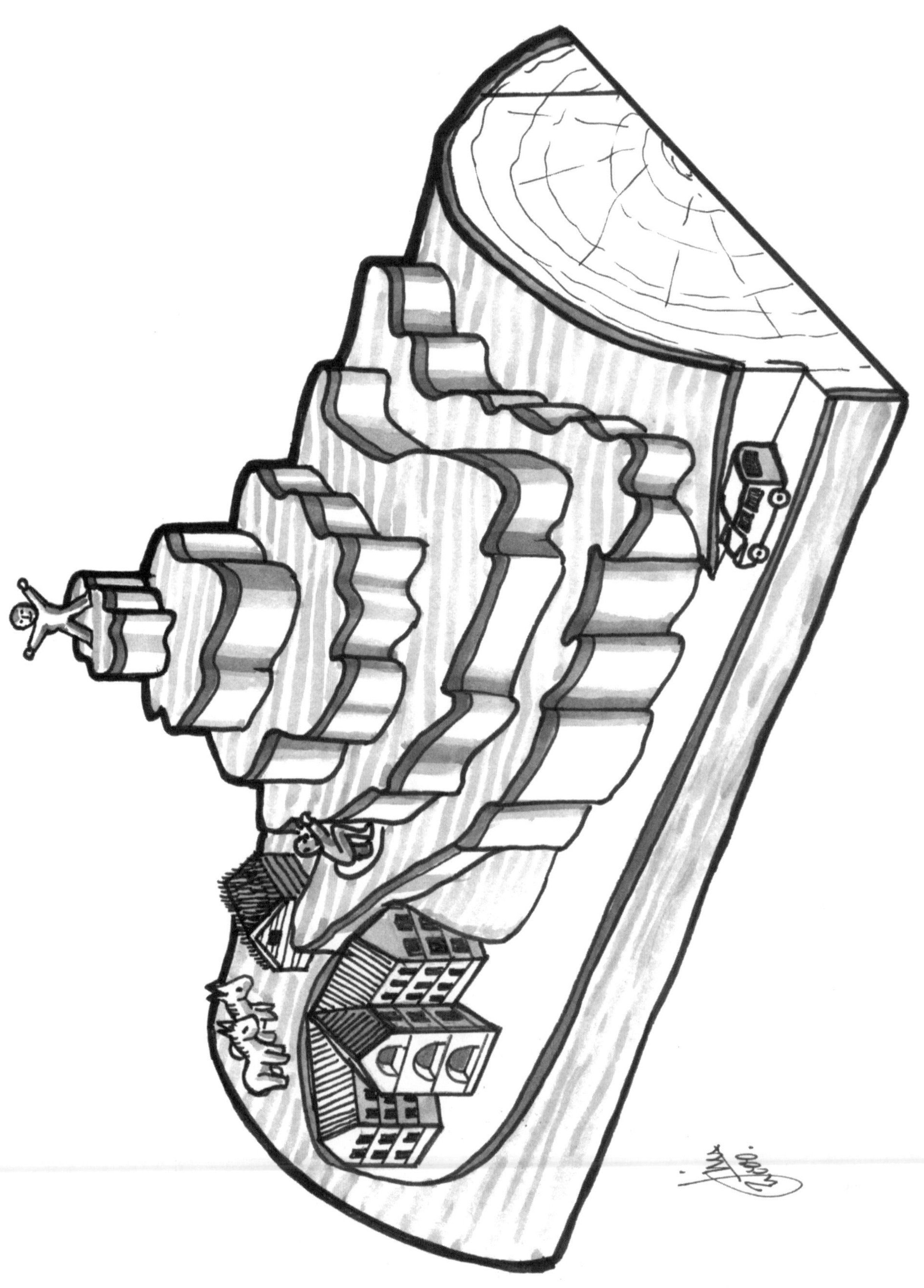

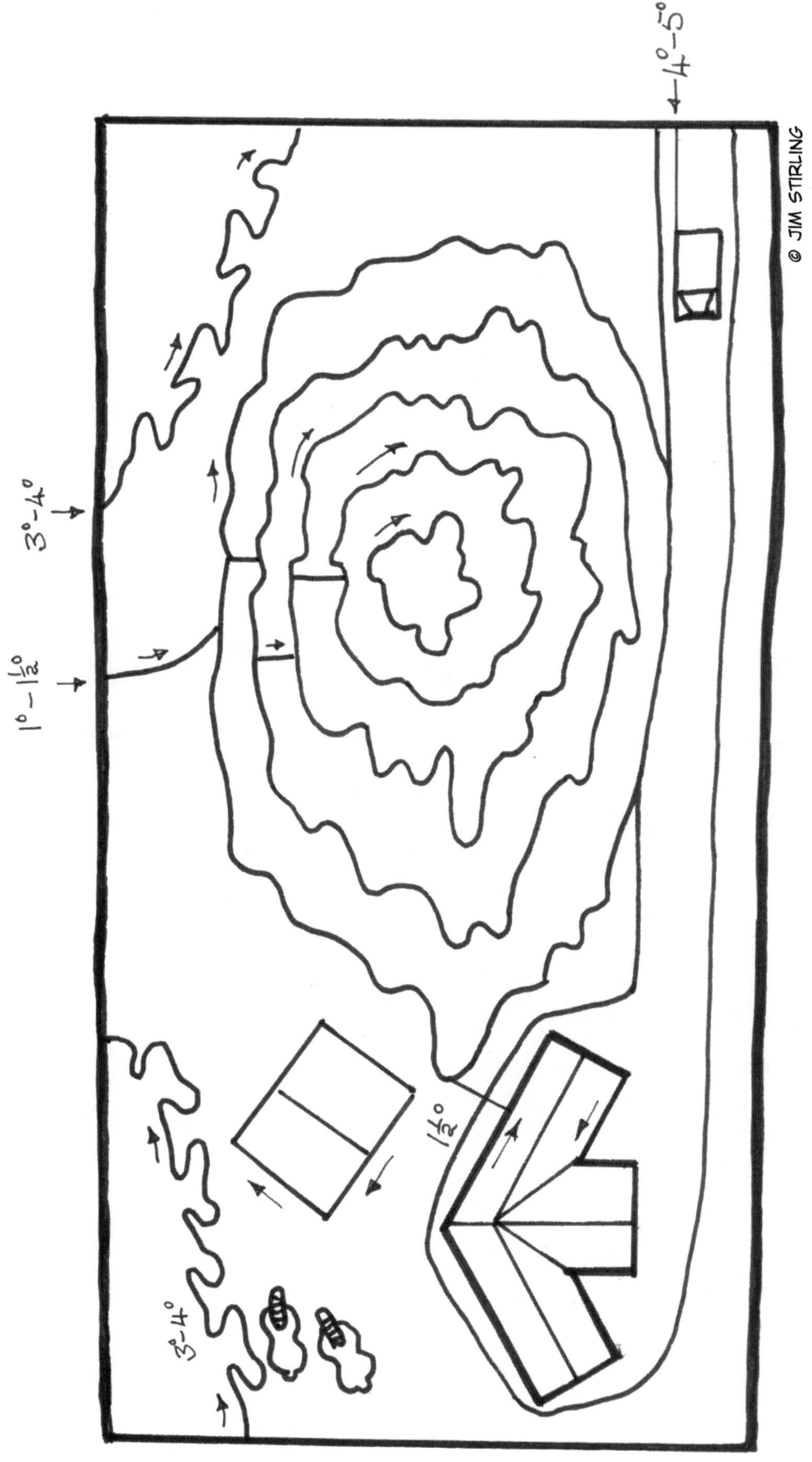
4°-5°
3°-4°
1°-1½°
2°
3°-4°
© JIM STIRLING

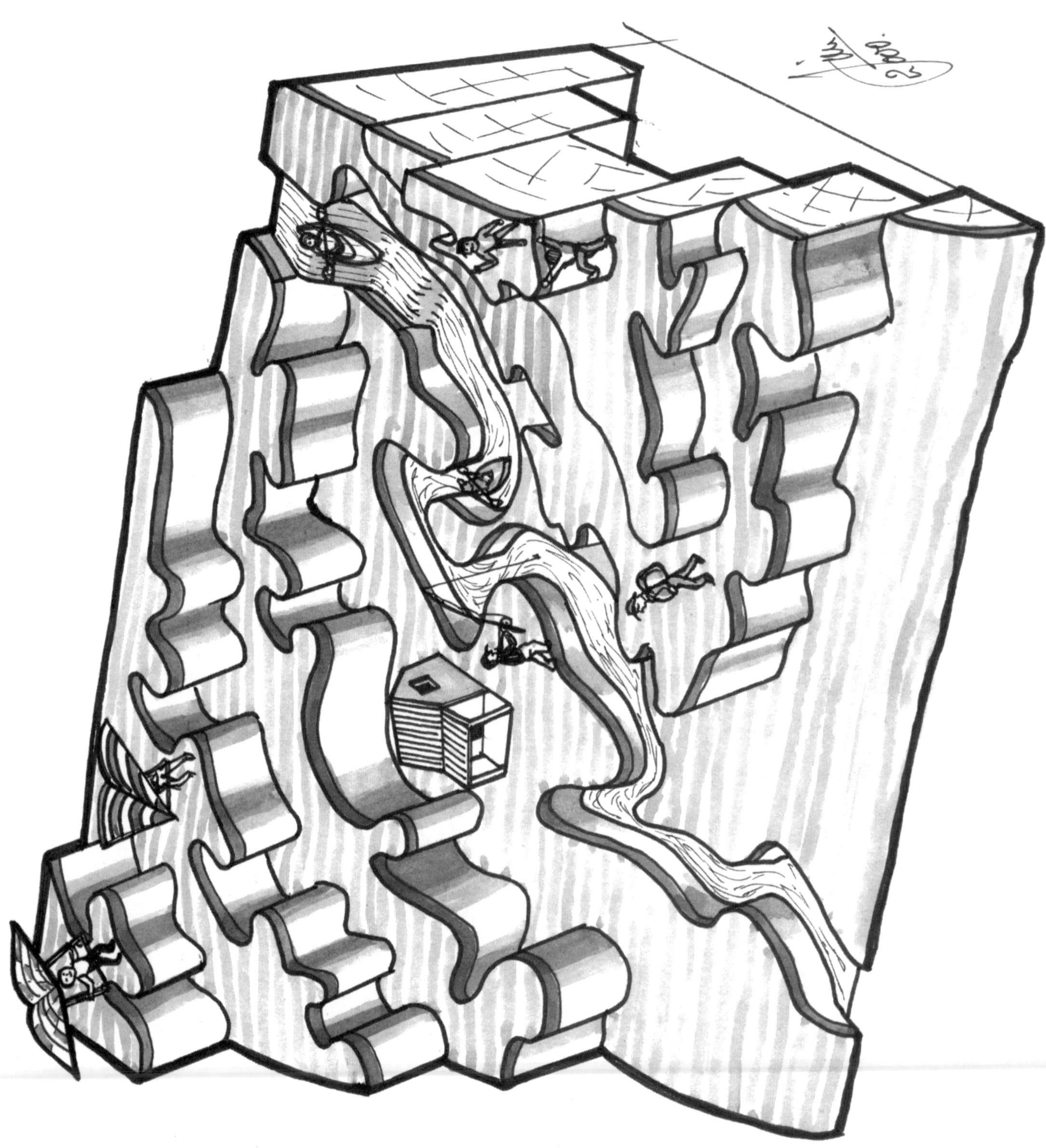

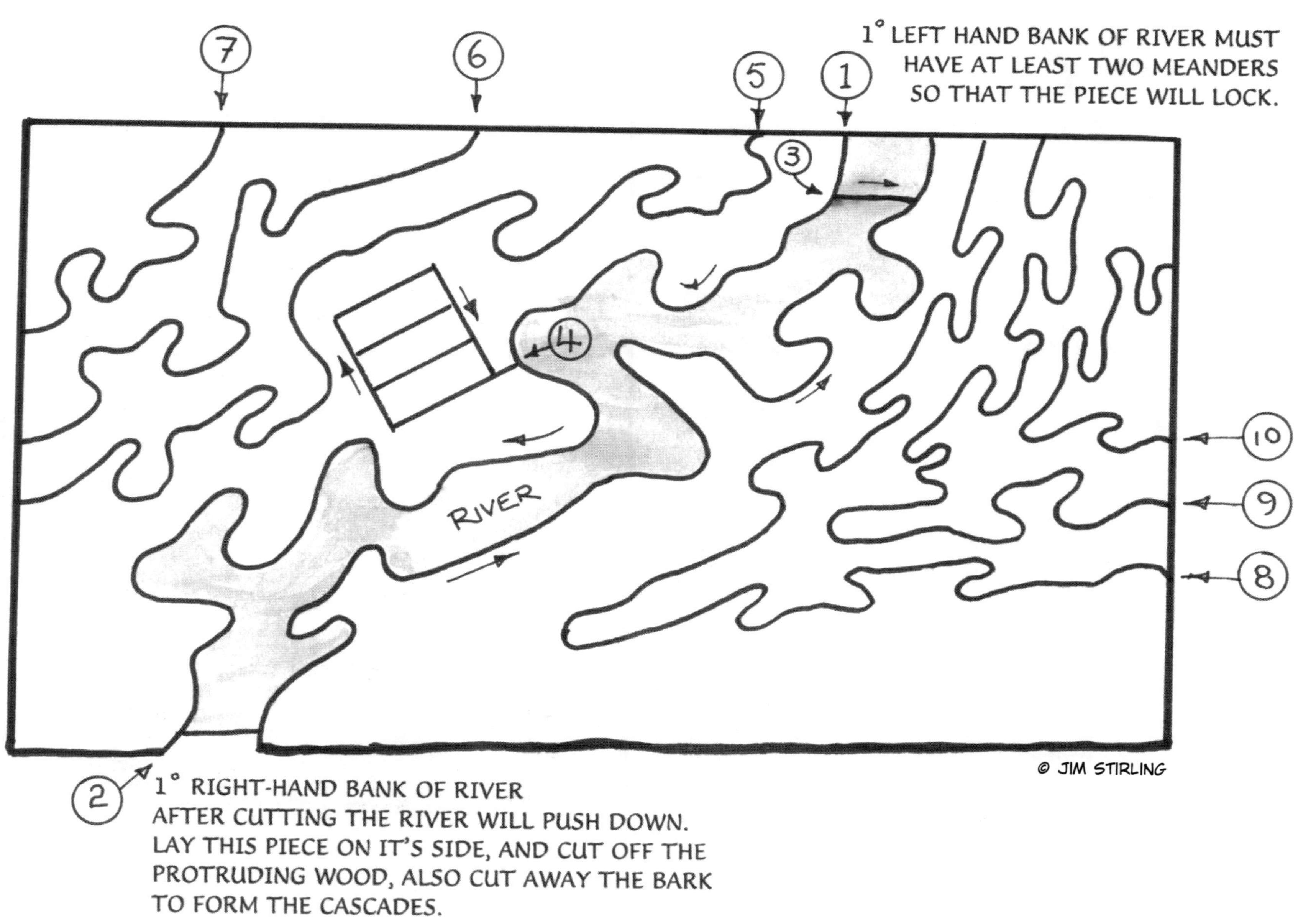
1° LEFT HAND BANK OF RIVER MUST
HAVE AT LEAST TWO MEANDERS
SO THAT THE PIECE WILL LOCK.
7
6
5
1
3
4
RIVER
10
9
8
1° RIGHT-HAND BANK OF RIVER
AFTER CUTTING THE RIVER WILL PUSH DOWN.
LAY THIS PIECE ON IT'S SIDE, AND CUT OFF THE
PROTRUDING WOOD, ALSO CUT AWAY THE BARK
TO FORM THE CASCADES.
2
© JIM STIRLING
SCROLL SAW CASTLES

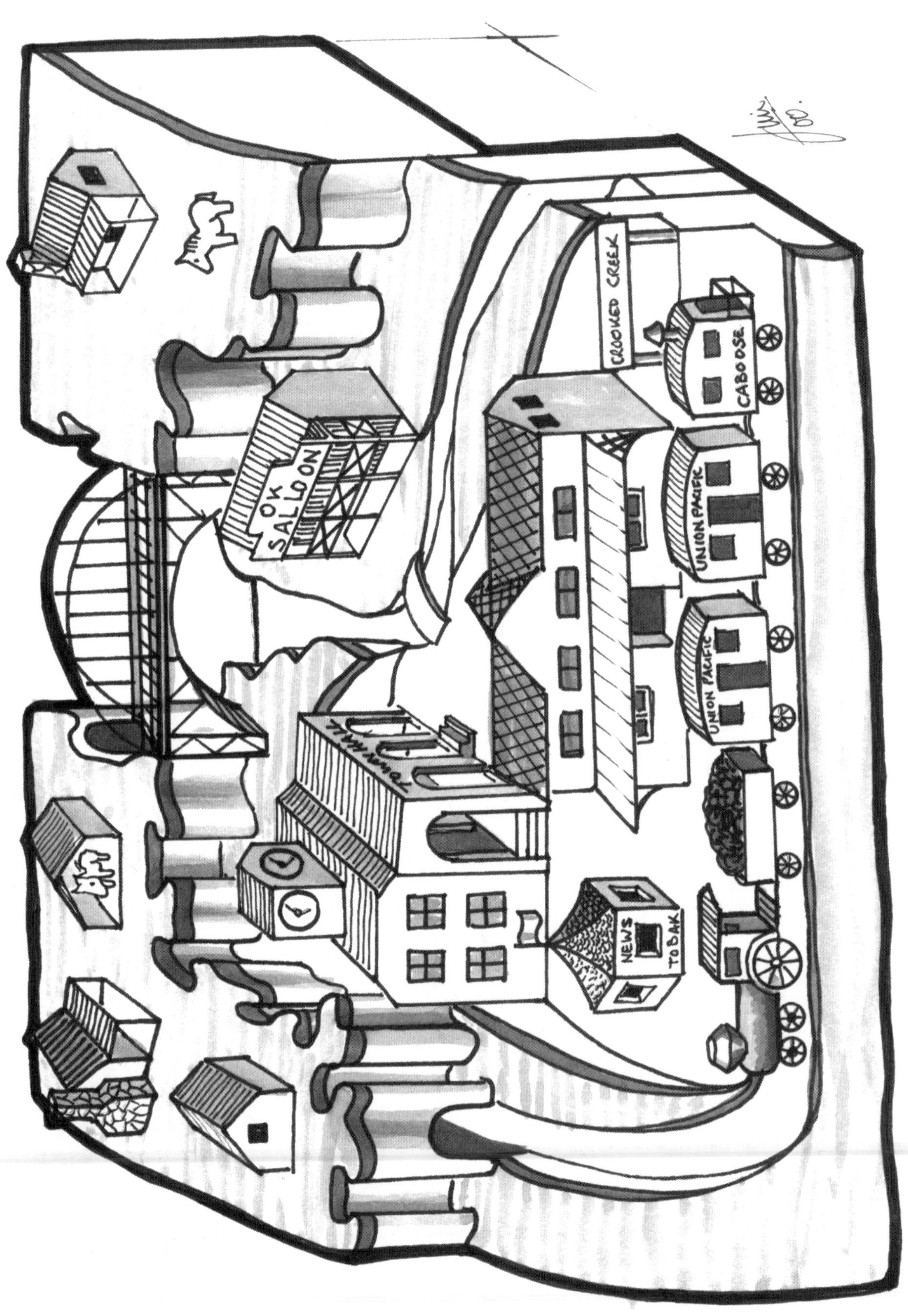
CROOKED CREEK
CABOOSE
UNION PACIFIC
UNION PACIFIC
OK SALOON
NEWS
TOBAK

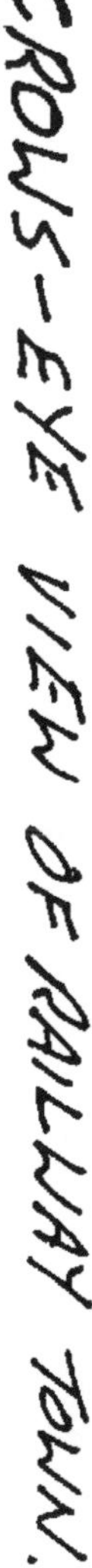

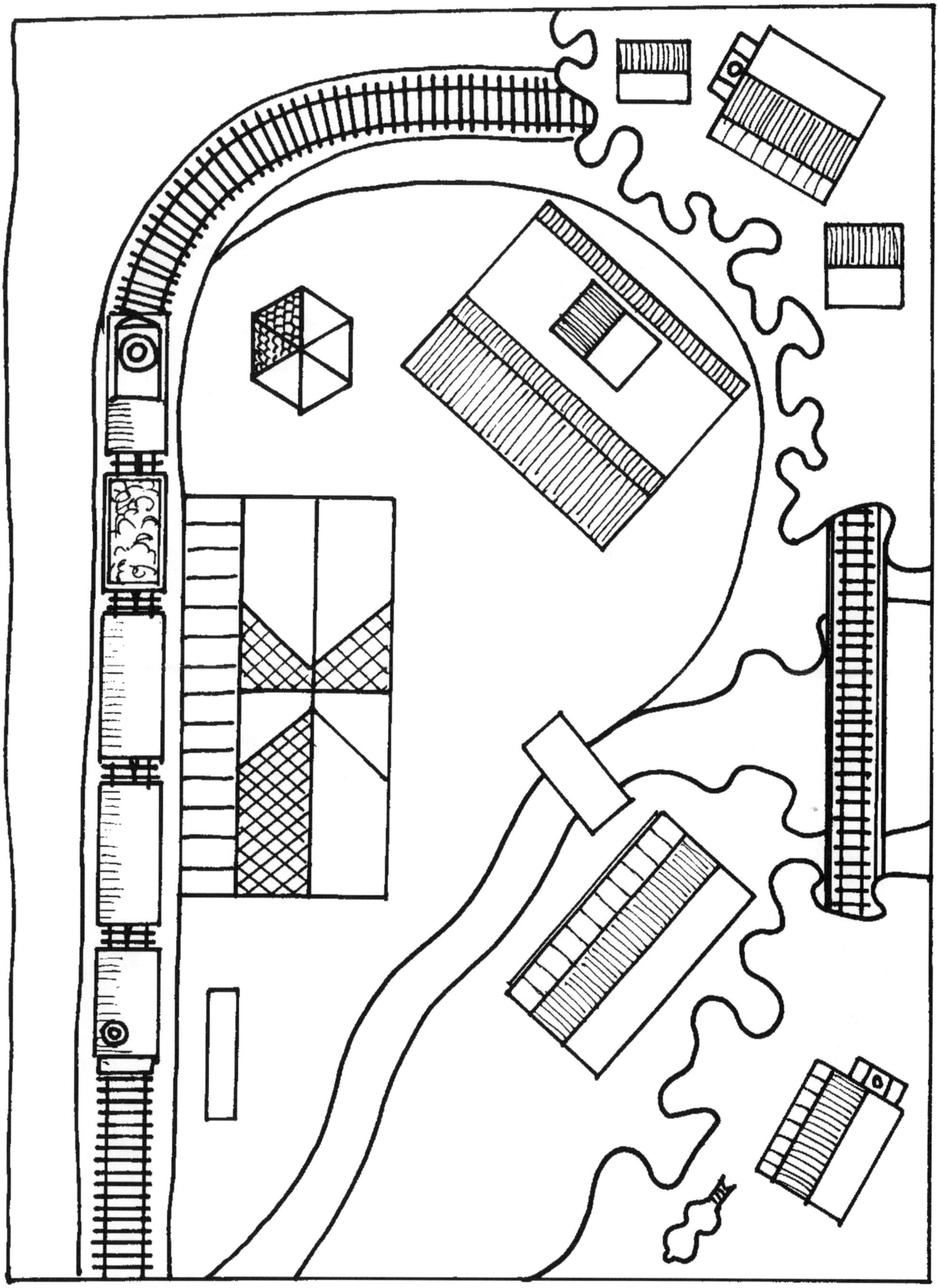

© JIM STIRLING

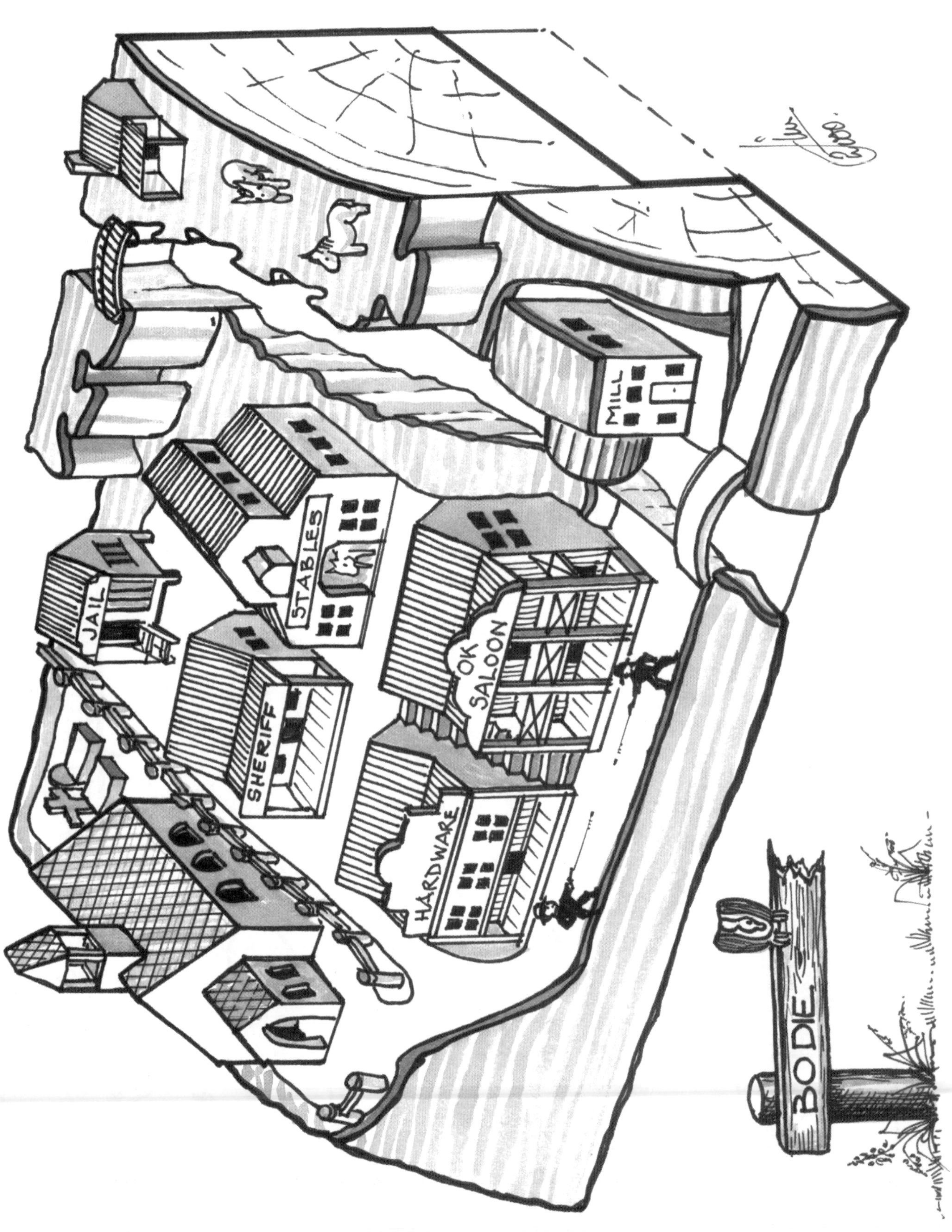
MILL
STABLES
JAIL
SHERIFF
OK
SALOON
HARDWARE
BODIE

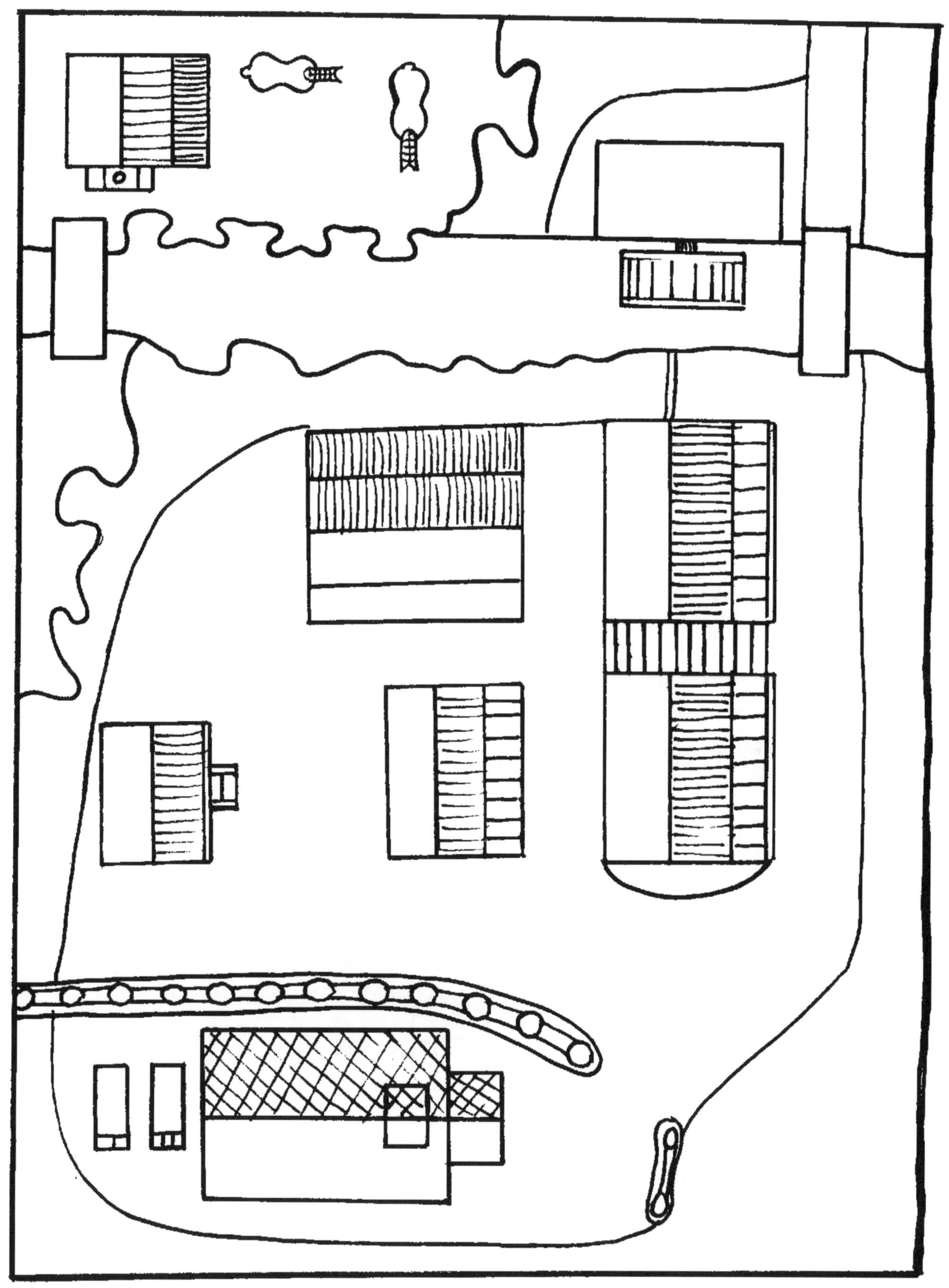

© JIM STIRLING

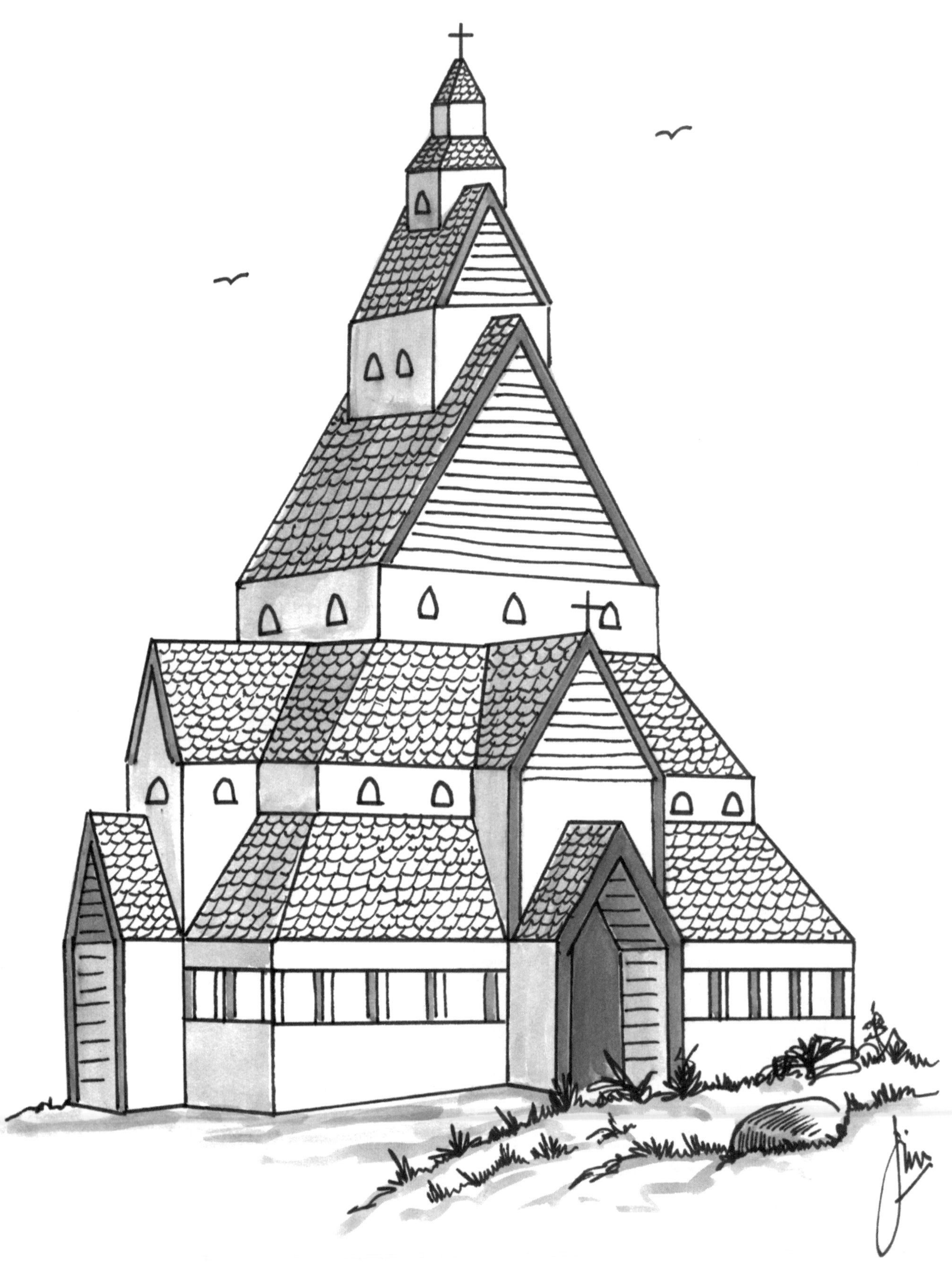

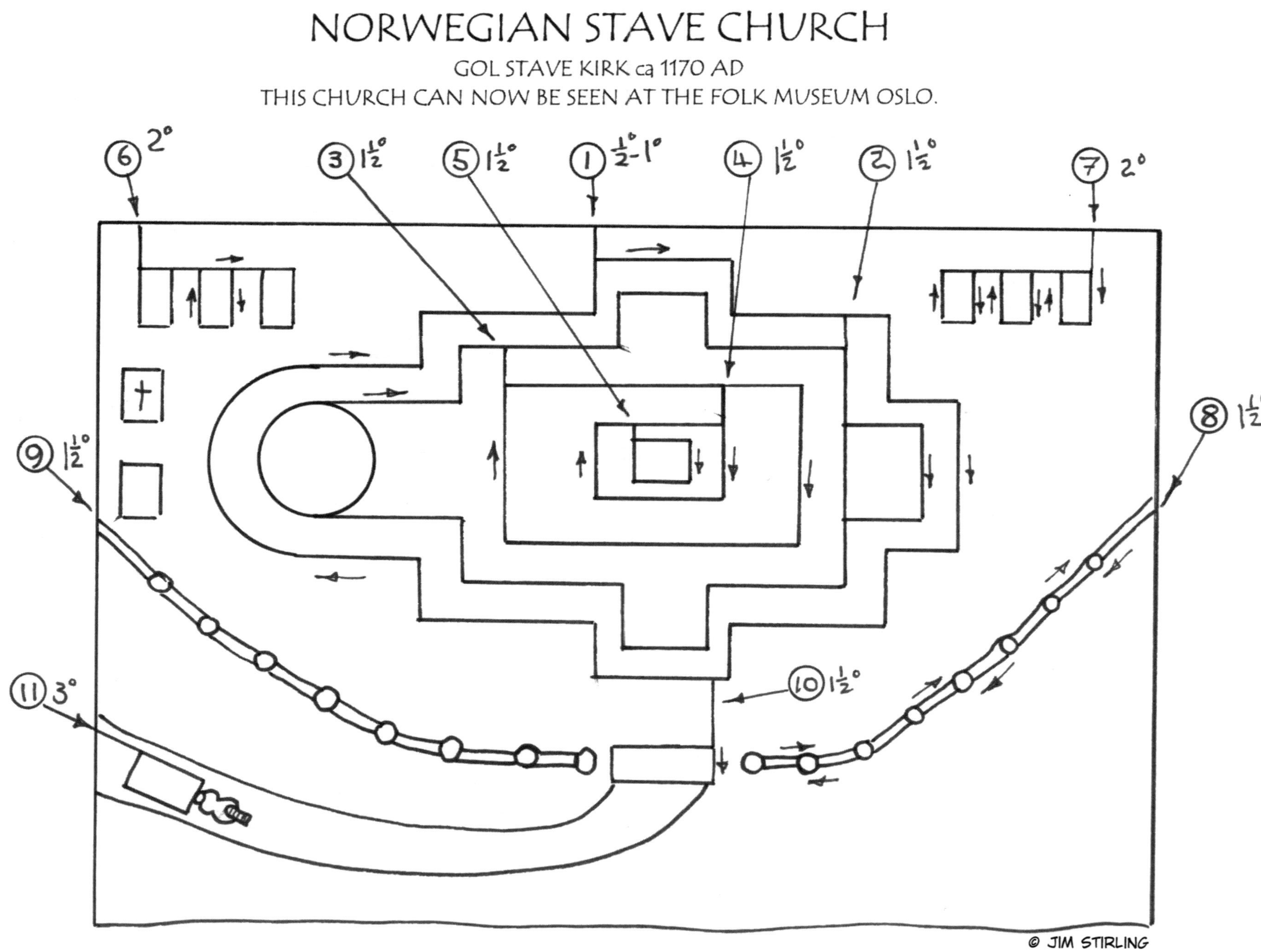

NORWEGIAN STAVE CHURCH
GOL STAVE KIRK ca 1170 AD
THIS CHURCH CAN NOW BE SEEN AT THE FOLK MUSEUM OSLO.
© JIM STIRLING
SCROLL SAW CASTLES

NORWEGIAN STAVE CHURCH

GOL STAVE CHURCH CA 1170 AD
THIS CHURCH CAN NOW BE SEEN AT THE FOLK MUSEUM OSLO

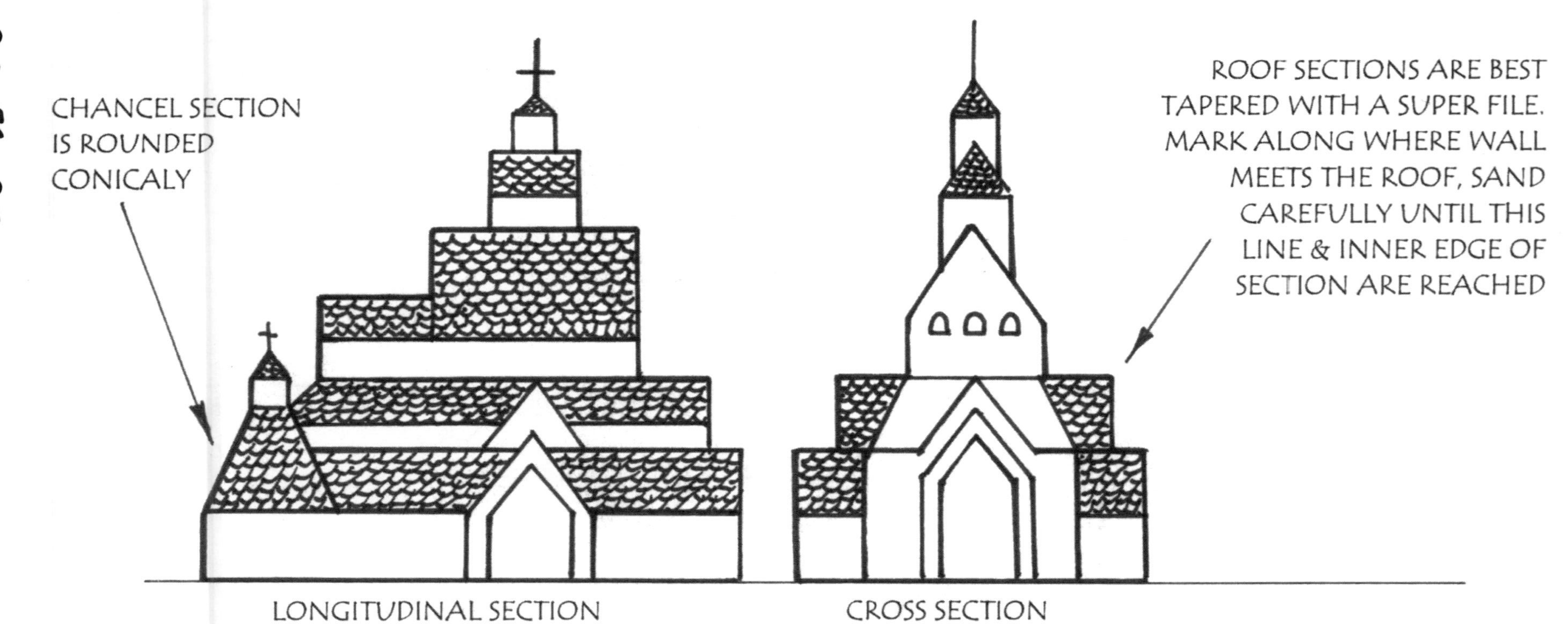

Moon Colony
Pattern

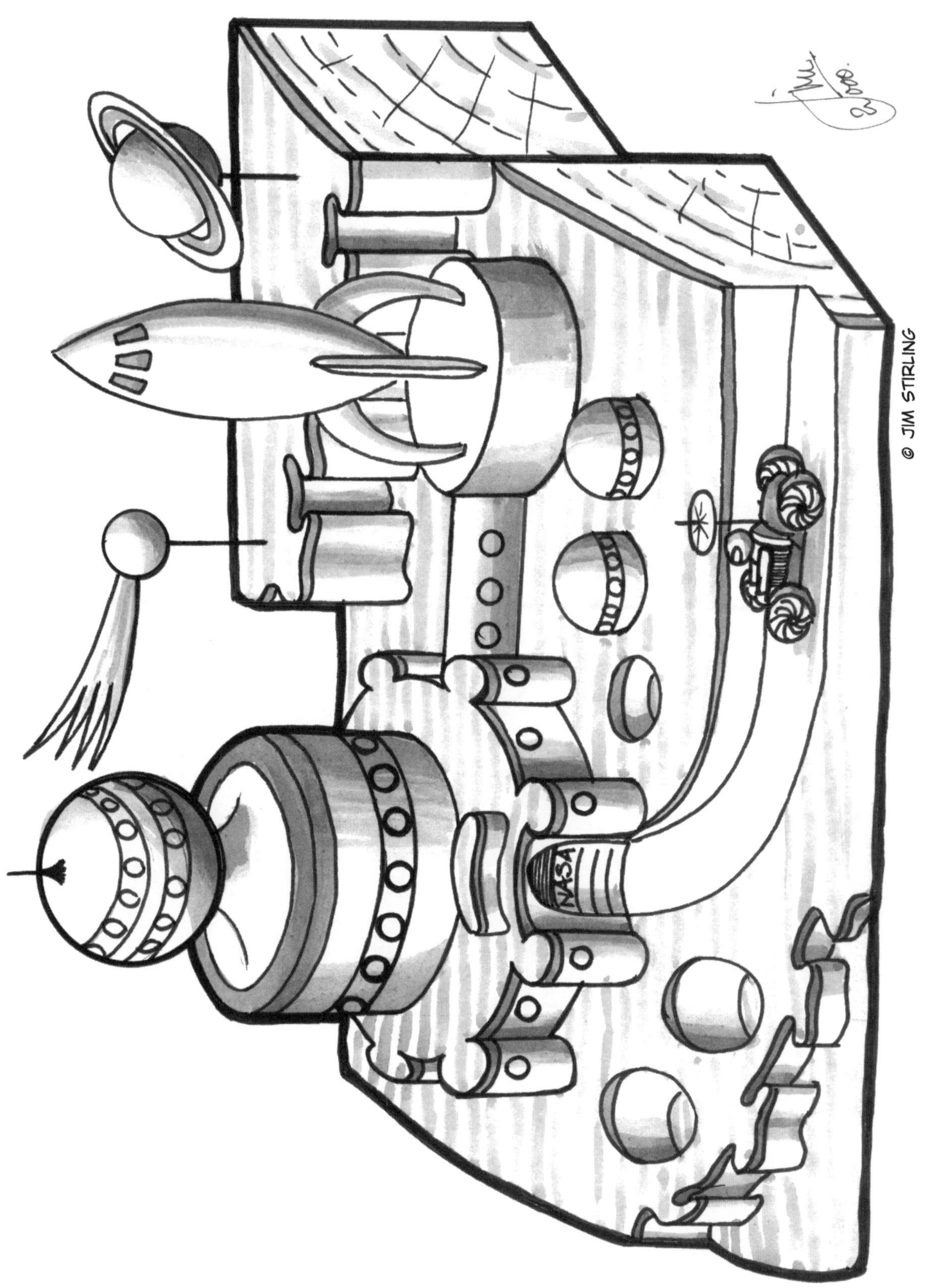

MOON ROCKET DETAILS

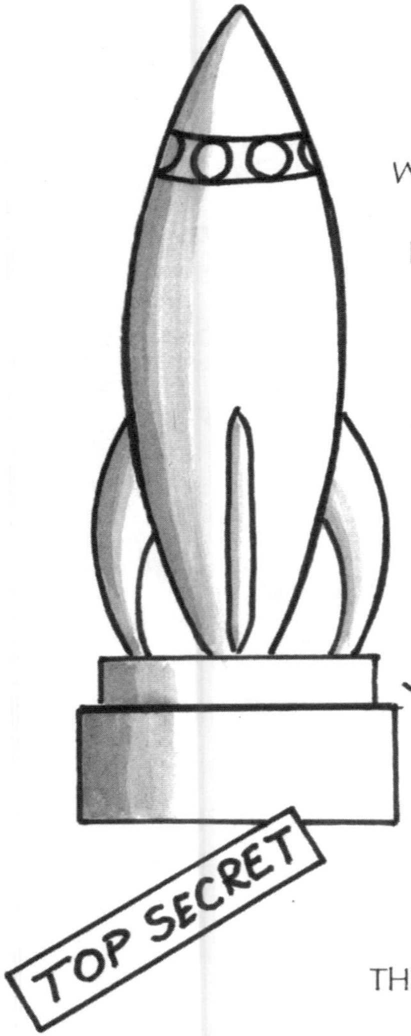

BURN LINES WITH WIRE WHILST PIECE IS SPINNING ON THE LATHE. BURN ROUND WINDOWS WITH SPECIAL IRON IN PYROGRAPHY TOOL.

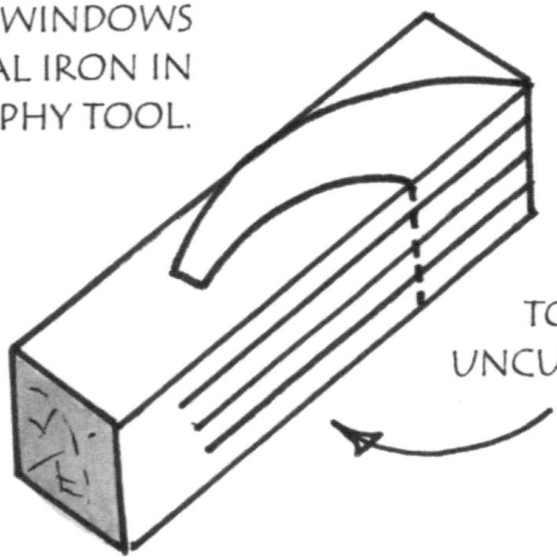

ALL FOUR FINS ON THE ROCKET ARE CUT AT ONCE. SLICE INTO STOCK MAKING CUTS TO MAKE THE FINS. LEAVE SOME OF THE STOCK UNCUT. TRACE FIN SHAPE ON THE TOP & CUT OUT.

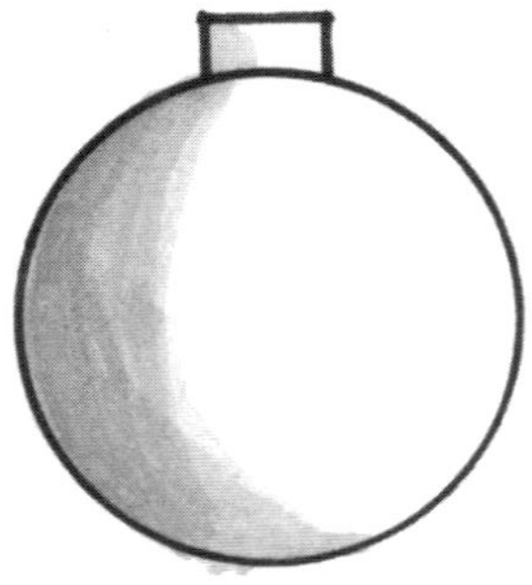

TURN ROCKET FROM SPARE STOCK, LEAVING IT STANDING ON A BASE. GLUE FINS IN PLACE. THEN GLUE ONTO CONICAL CUT BASE FROM MODEL.

ALL-ROUND TOWERS AND BASES MUST BE CUT WITH A LUG PROTRUDING. THIS IS TO STOP THE PIECE FROM TWISTING IN THE MODEL. IT CAN BE CUT OFF AT GROUND LEVEL OR MADE INTO AN INTEGRAL FEATURE OF THE MODEL.

USE MELTED GLUE TO SECURE PIECE ONTO
ROUND STOCK MOUNTED ONTO FACEPLATE.

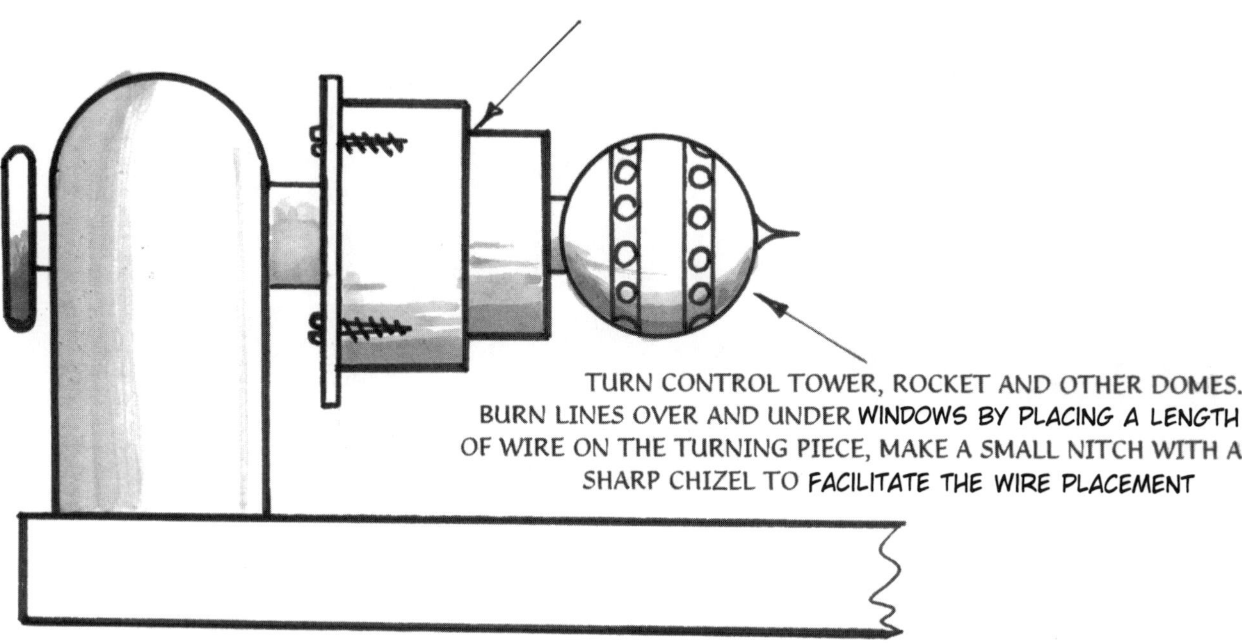

TURN CONTROL TOWER, ROCKET AND OTHER DOMES.
BURN LINES OVER AND UNDER WINDOWS BY PLACING A LENGTH
OF WIRE ON THE TURNING PIECE, MAKE A SMALL NITCH WITH A
SHARP CHIZEL TO FACILITATE THE WIRE PLACEMENT

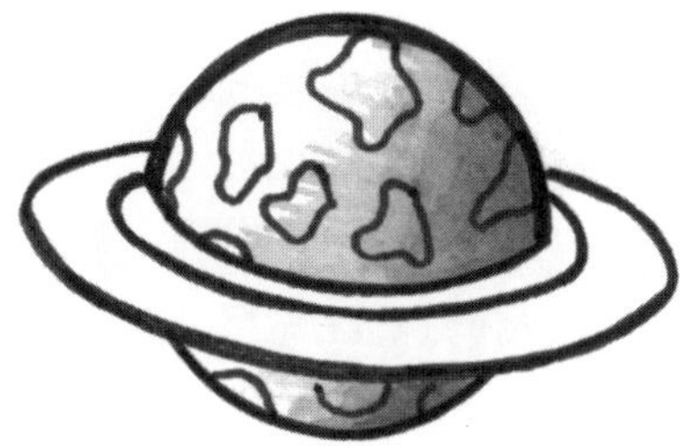

PLANETS CAN BE TURNED ON THE LATHE
THEY CAN BE COLOURED WITH FELT TIPPED
MARKERS WHILST SPINNING. THE RINGS ON
SATURN CAN BE BANDED WITH DIFFERENT COLOURS.

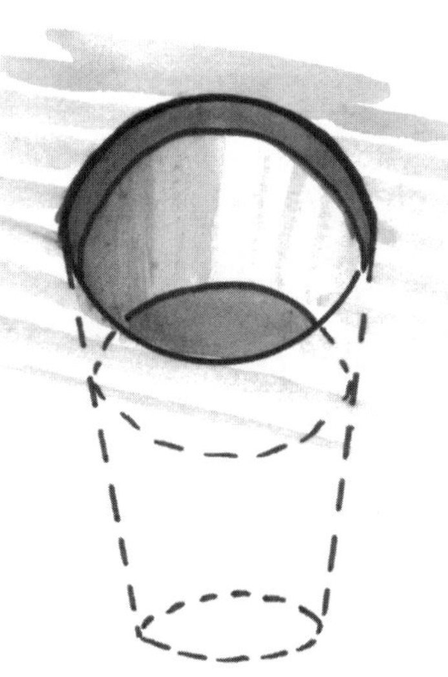

CRATERS ARE MADE BY SETTING
TABLE ON 3° - 4°AND CUTTING
ANTICLOCKWISE THE PROTRUDING
PART IS THEN CUTOFF FLUSH WITH
THE UNDERSIDE OF MODEL.